Psychic Telemetry:
New Key to
Health, Wealth and Perfect Living

Psychic Telemetry: New Key to Health, Wealth and Perfect Living

Robert A. Ferguson

Unity Library & Archives
1901 NW Blue Parkway
Unity Village, MO 64065

PARKER PUBLISHING COMPANY, INC.   **WEST NYACK, NEW YORK**

© 1977 by
Parker Publishing Company, Inc.
West Nyack, New York

*All rights reserved. No part of this book
may be reproduced in any form or by any
means, without permission in writing from
the publisher.*

This book is a reference work based on research by
the author. The opinions expressed herein are not
necessarily those of or endorsed by the Publisher.

Library of Congress Cataloging in Publication Data

Ferguson, Robert A
   Psychic telemetry.

   1. Success. 2. Psychical research. I. Title.
BJ1611.2.F46   131'.32   77-24319
ISBN 0-13-732388-3

Printed in the United States of America

To Cindy, Rob, and Velma
for bringing so much happiness into the world

WHAT THIS BOOK CAN DO FOR YOU

Is there something in your life that needs changing for the better? Do you need more money? Are you seeking true love and romance? Do you wonder what your purpose in life is? Are you growing old too quickly? Are you suffering from poor health? Do you have talents that go unnoticed by others? Do you want to know what the future holds, and be able to change it?

You no longer need to feel the frustration of wishes unfulfilled. This book will change your life as no other book before it.

Long before you reach the end of this book you will be changing your life for the better. The more I became exposed to the unnecessary frustration many people experience in learning personal psychic development, the stronger became my desire to make a common sense, personal development book available to *you*.

There are literally hundreds of case histories that I could cite in the Introduction of this book. I become so excited over the success of my friends and students that have used *Psychic Telemetry* that my thoughts trip over one another as I attempt to write of only a few of the "miracles" that have changed so many lives—Miracles that will change *your* life as well.

"Plain Jane" laid down her mop and broom to become a fashion model. Hammon D. didn't have a chance to win a political office, and yet he was elected County Supervisor. When Albert V. thought his love life was a thing of the past, he found the perfect marriage partner. Unhappy Sally turned the tables on her evil tormentors and became, in her words, "the happiest girl in the world." Bob F. thought his Mexican vacation was a disaster. He was far from home and out of money. He bet his last two dollars at the dog racing track. He walked away with $576.

PSYCHIC TELEMETRY POWER IS REAL

I make no false nor unfounded claims of *Psychic Telemetry* Power, I don't have to. *Psychic Telemetry* is real and it proves itself—miracle after miracle.

I have personally taught hundreds of people how to use *Psychic Telemetry* power to bring health, wealth and happiness into their lives. At other times, I have taught *Psychic Telemetry* over television with equal success.

I have taken those very same psychic lessons that have proved so successful for others, and compiled them into this easy-to-use, and easy-to-understand book.

Many of my students have suggested that I title this book of instruction, *The Miracle Book*. I do teach you to perform miracles. Long before you have completed *Psychic Telemetry's* first chapter, miracles will be happening to you everyday.

Psychic Telemetry Power is real. Thousands of people are using its power at this very moment, and *you*, too, should be one of those miracle workers. Do you want to go from poverty to riches? Do you want to experience a miraculous healing? You can, and you will. *Psychic Telemetry* never fails the honest seeker.

HOW DAVE E. WISHED $2,000 INTO HIS LIFE OVERNIGHT

Dave E., of Denver, Colorado, was ready to begin his first year at the University when he attended his first *Psychic Telemetry* class.

"I haven't been able to find a job this summer," Dave told the *Psychic Telemetry* group. "I only have three days left before I have to pay my first year's tuition at the University, and I don't have a cent."

What this Book Can Do for You

Dave's world appeared bleak and hopeless. It looked like his dream was going to turn into a nightmare. But that was before Dave knew how to use his *Psychic Telemetry* power.

Before the *Psychic Telemetry* class adjourned for the evening, Dave was shown how to perform the *Psychic Telemetry* Prosperity Ritual. Dave was the first one to class the next evening. His face was wreathed in smiles.

"This probably won't surprise you, but I have just received $2,000—more than enough to pay for my tuition."

A miracle? Not really. Just a very average example of the power of *Psychic Telemetry* to change the course of events to *your* favor.

Dave had performed his Prosperity Ritual at about 9:00 P.M. At 8:00 A.M., the following morning, Dave's telephone rang. It was Maurice. Maurice M. was a successful corporation executive, and an old friend of Dave's deceased father.

"Dave? This is Maurice," the voice boomed over the telephone. "I just felt like I had to call you. Years ago, I promised your father that I would see to it that you would go to college. Are you short of tuition money?"

Dave hesitated before he admitted that, yes, he was short of money. "I need $1,200," he told Maurice.

"I'll send you $2,000 right now, and you can expect more in the future," Maurice said.

Thanks to *Psychic Telemetry's* Prosperity Enchantments, Dave E. is now a well-known, prosperous, criminal attorney.

EVERYONE HAS PSYCHIC TELEMETRY POWER

It's true! Everyone does have *Psychic Telemetry* power. But it's equally true that very few people use this magical power—maybe one person in a thousand.

There are many reasons for the reluctance of these people to delve into the occult. Most of the objections are downright silly, based upon superstitions from the ignorant past.

There is only one difference between a successful, happy person and an unhappy, frustrated person. The successful person uses occult principles, either consciously or unconsciously. Unsuccessful people do not use *Psychic Telemetry* power, either because they fear it, or they have not been fortunate enough to learn of its miraculous powers.

PSYCHIC TELEMETRY IS NOT A NEW OR MYSTERIOUS POWER

What awesome power did the saints and sages of the ancient races of man possess? To what power do we attribute the miracles of the alchemist and the prophets of the Middle Ages? It was *Psychic Telemetry*. The very power that I will teach you to use in this book.

The wise men of these ages past wrote their secrets in a manner to confuse the layman. Much of what they wrote, and the tools they required to perform their miracles were unnecessary.

This book has been written in a simple and easy-to-follow method. There is no guessing, and no false starts. I have stripped the unnecessary mumbo-jumbo from the Enchantments and Rituals to present you with a clear and concise method of performing realistic miracles.

HOW A CALIFORNIA POLICEWOMAN USED PSYCHIC TELEMETRY TO APPREHEND CRIMINALS AND GAINED A PROMOTION

Fern H. knew that she would have a tough job ahead when she entered the Police Academy. Fern relished the thought of law enforcement, but she knew that she would have to prove herself to her male peers—and she did!

Fern's first assignment was in the apprehension of shop lifters. "Not a very challenging assignment," she said.

Using Psychic Telemetry techniques, Fern herself had soon arrested more shop lifters than an entire team of detectives combined. But Fern still dreamed of a more active assignment. Fern performed a *Psychic Telemetry* Ritual and "saw" an attempted bank robbery days before it happened. Fern was ready.

What this Book Can Do for You

Fully informed of the coming robbery, Fern stationed herself inside the bank doors. Single-handedly she disarmed and arrested the would-be robber.

Fern has received many citations for bravery since those days. She is now one of the top female law enforcement officials in the world.

"I use *Psychic Telemetry* everyday in my work," she wrote. "If it wasn't for my psychic powers, I would still be sitting at a police desk answering the telephone."

I have hundreds of letters from people just like Fern. Letters from people who are prosperous and successful—thanks to *Psychic Telemetry*.

YOUR EVERY WISH CAN BECOME A POSITIVE REALITY

There is no need to feel frustrated. *Psychic Telemetry* can give you health, wealth and happiness.

Psychic Telemetry "wishes" are not unrealistic hopes, they are positive commands. And what you command *does* happen. You can count positively on tangible results from your psychic desires.

Psychic Telemetry can turn your world away from poverty, ill health and loneliness, and replace them with wealth, health and all of the love you can handle.

HOW TORU N.'S CRIPPLING ARTHRITIS "DISAPPEARED" OVERNIGHT

Toru N. was a prosperous and happy Japanese businessman. He had everything in the world that he had ever wanted, except freedom from pain.

Toru was wealthy. He and his wife had travelled to every continent on the globe. Without effort, Toru's business made more money than he could ever hope to spend.

Suddenly, and without warning, Toru was crippled by painful, and incurable arthritis. His wealth meant nothing. Toru was heard to say, "I would give every yen I have if I could be relieved of my terrible pain."

Luckily, a *Psychic Telemetry* student in Australia heard of Toru's plight, and flew to Osaka, Japan.

The *Psychic Telemetry* student met with Toru and his family. Together, they performed Psychic Medi-Telemetry Rituals. Toru later wrote:

> "I didn't have much confidence in the healing Rituals, but I was willing to try anything. I knew that if I didn't receive relief from my arthritis soon, that I would commit suicide.
>
> "I didn't sleep much the night of the healing Rituals. I kept feeling a warm sensation running up and down my arms, legs, and my spine. Toward dawn, I drifted off to sleep.
>
> "I had had little sleep during my painful affliction, and when I was still sleeping in the early afternoon, my wife became concerned and shook me awake. I had been sleeping as soundly as a baby. I felt wonderful.
>
> "I couldn't believe that I was awake. 'I must be dreaming,' I said to my wife. 'My arthritis is cured!' I jumped from my bed and ran shouting about the house. 'A miracle! A miracle!'
>
> "I had been bed-ridden for one full year and had spent thousands of yen on medical doctors.
>
> "It took but one hour of *Psychic Telemetry's* powerful healing Rituals to cure what had defied the most competent men of medical science."

Phillip, the Australian healer returned to his home, content that he had been able to remove Toru's chronic affliction. He was later happily surprised to learn that the grateful Toru had set up a generous trust fund in his name. Phillip will never have to work at a job for as long as he lives.

This true case history is not exceptional, nor is it a miracle. It is an example of the positive results that you can expect from all of your *Psychic Telemetry* Rituals. *You* can do this exact same thing, and even more.

YOUR PSYCHIC TELEMETRY POWER
IS ANXIOUS TO GO TO WORK

Your ever present psychic power has been laying dormant below the surface of your conscious mind, but it has now been activated.

You have been doing more than just reading the words from the pages of this *Psychic Telemetry* introduction. You have been opening your mind, and allowing your innate psychic power to flow to the surface of your consciousness. It wants to go to work. It's anxious to perform miracles—not only for you, but for your family and friends as well.

I make no claims that when you finish this book that a "psychic veil" will be lifted. I make the claim that there is no psychic veil to be lifted. I make the claim that you have this great psychic power *before* you read this book.

Psychic Telemetry was written especially for *you*. *Psychic Telemetry* is a sturdy guide that directs you in the proper use of Rituals, Enchantments, and healing secrets so that your every wish may come true.

Spend a few minutes each day recalling some of the words from this book and its many valuable chapters. You will become anything you want to be, and have anything you want to have.

Robert A. Ferguson

TABLE OF CONTENTS

Chapter One — Psychic Telemetry Has Reaped Miracles for Others - Just as it Can for You (17)

You Have Already Experienced Simple Psychic Telemetry (18) The Great Mystics Vanished, But Their Powers Survive (19) The Pillars of Power Have Now Been Rediscovered (20) Intuition—Your Psychic Legacy from Ages Past (21) How to Unlock the Mighty Force of Your First Pillar of Power (22) Alex R. Clung to a Worthless Parcel of Texas Prairie—Oil was Discovered (23) You Can Do What Alex Did—And Far More (24) The Subconscious Mind is the Cosmic Mind (25) How Your Cosmic Mind Speaks to You (25) This Psychic Power is Not Determined By Age, Sex, or Religion (26) How Allen F. Won $800 at the Craptable After Using the Pillar of Power Magic Ritual (26) The Second Great Pillar of Power is Yours to Command (28) The Genius of Long Gone Souls is at Your Fingertips (28) How to Create Your Own Guardian Genie (29) Where to Begin (29) The Guardian Genie Creation Ritual (30) How to Use Your Guardian Genie to Fulfill Your Every Command (31) Lorraine T. Purchased the Desert Land. Her Guardian Genie Found the Water (31) Ritual of the Second Pillar of Power (32) Psychic Telemetry Always Helps—It Never Harms (33)

Chapter Two — Psychic Telemetry Enchantments That Automatically Bring You Floodtides of Cash, Treasure, and Security (35)

Psychic Telemetry's Initiation Ritual (36) Be Your Own Secret Society (37) Powerful Enchantment for Winning Contests (37) How Agnes C. Won Over $500,000 with the Enchantment for Winning Contests (37) How to Perform Your Enchantment

Psychic Telemetry Enchantments That Automatically Bring You Floodtides of Cash, Treasure, and Security (con't)

Ritual (39) Enchantment for Personal Recognition (40) How Larry X. Went from Clerk to Engineering Specialist (40) Psychic Telemetry Enchantments Work Best When Used for Good (42) Enchantment for Health (43) How Lester W. Conquered His Migraine Headaches By Using the Enchantment for Health (43) This Magical Enchantment Will Give You Power Over Others (44) How Hammon D. Was Elected County Supervisor (44) Enchantment That Will Let You Know What Others are Thinking (45) How Cindy F. Used the Enchantment to Know What Others Were Thinking to Earn $500 a Month from Her Hobby (45) Enchantment to Make Yourself Desirable (47) How Albert V. Found a Perfect Partner (47) General Enchantment for Prosperity (48) How Derek J. Went from Wishful Thinker to Company President (48) Mary D. Needed $400. She Performed Her Enchantment and Had the Money in 45 Minutes (49) Enchantment to Increase Self-Esteem (50) How "Plain Jane" Became a Fashion Model (50) Enchantment for Protection from Evil (51) How the Enchantment Against Evil Turned the Tables on Sally's Tormentor (52) Enchantments Work Exciting Miracles (53)

Chapter Three — How Visual-Telemetry Will Give You the Magnetic King Midas Golden Gaze (55)

Gary U.'s King Midas Gold Gaze Made Him One of America's Newest Millionaires! (55) Visual-Telemetry—A Look Into the Future (58) Rituals of the Visions (61) How Dorothy K. Recovered an $8,000 Loan That She Thought Was Lost Forever (63) Visual-Telemetry and the Role of Meditation (64) Everyone Has Visual-Telemetry Power But Few Use It (65) Curtis H. Watched a Missouri Tornado from His California Living Room (66) How a Psychic Telemetry Worker Operates (69) Do Some People Have More Visual-Telemetry Power Than Others? (69)

Chapter Four — How to Read Telemetric Sign Language from the Cosmic Mind (71)

How Steve R. Saw an Upcoming Vacancy at His Place of Work and Gained a Big Promotion (72) Cosmic Mind Speaks in Symbols, Not in Words (74) Telemetric Sign Language is Easy (74) How to Know What is Happening Anywhere in the World (75) How to Read Telemetric Sign Language (75) Telemetric Sign Language is Simple to Learn (79) How to Begin Your Telemetric

Table of Contents 13

> How to Read Telemetric Sign Language from the Cosmic Mind (con't)

Language Lesson (79) How to Begin Using Your Telemetric Sign Language (80) The Telemetric Sign Language Ritual (81) Ryan R. Used Telemetric Sign Language to Predict a New Discovery in Astronomy (81) How to Differentiate Between Symbolic Pictures and Actual Events (82) Sensory-Telemetry (83) How Joachim V. Thwarted the Attempts of a Vicious Co-Worker to Have Him Dismissed from His Well-Paying Job (83) How to Use Sensory Telemetry (84) The Sensory-Telemetry Power Ritual (84) Sensory-Telemetry is Your Caution Light Against Danger (85) When Medical Science Failed, Gordon P. Used Sensory-Telemetry to Diagnose His Own Illness (85) How Audio-Telemetry Told Judy G. Where to Find Her Missing Child (87) How to Use Audio-Telemetry (89) The Audio-Telemetry Ritual (90) Use Your New Powers to Make Every Dream Come True (90)

Chapter Five — How to Command and Control Others with the Magic Tele-Aurascope (91)

Jeffrey B. Soared from Underpaid Teacher to Top Educational Administrator (91) The Ritual That Will Direct the Magic Tele-Aurascope (92) Louise L. Became the Best-Liked Girl in the Office and Married the Boss (92) How to Work with the Magic Tele-Aurascope (94) How Harlan V. Commanded an Instant Apology (94) Famous Movie Star Builds Wall of Protection (95) The Magic Tele-Aurascope's Law of Attraction (95) Zola H. Zooms from Welfare Mother to Successful Business Woman (96) How to See the Aura (97) Helen M. Wished to Be a Policewoman—Her Dream Came True (98) Alexis Catches a "Con" Man (98) How to Analyze the Human Aura (99) Table of Colors (99) Positive Red Tones (103) The Negative Red Tones (104) Spiritual Qualities Within the Aura (104) Characteristics of Those Possessing Positive Blue Tones (107) General Characteristics of Negative Blue Tones (108) Positive Qualities of Those Having Yellow as Their Dominant Color (112) The Negative Yellow Tones (112) The Glorious Green (113) Miscellaneous Aura Colors (115) Know All There is to Know About Every Person You Meet (116) How to Use Your Magic Tele-Aurascope to Make Others Do Your Bidding (116)

Chapter Six — Tele-Psychometry—Divining Miracle Power from Inanimate Objects (117)

How Inanimate Objects Talk to You (117) Harold C. Helps Police Solve Bizarre Murders (118) There is Much More to Harold's

Tele-Psychometry—Divining Miracle Power from Inanimate Objects (con't)

Story (120) The Power of Psychic-Telemetry Created Even More Miracles (121) Magic Words That Will Increase Your Tele-Psychometry Powers (122) Demitrius V. Earns Thousands of Dollars from Her Collection of Antiques (123) How Inanimate Objects "Talk" to You (125) How to "Read" the Past History of Any Inanimate Object (125) Inanimate Objects Can Be Powerful Forces for Evil (127) Iris S. Removed a Curse from a House and Made $50,000 in One Year (127) Iris Breaks the Evil Curse Upon the House (129) The Powerful Ritual That Will Banish Evil Influences from a House or Other Buildings (130) The Case of the Black Pentacle (132) Ritual of Exorcism to Banish Evil from Small Inanimate Objects (132) How to Build a Power That Attracts Good to Any Inanimate Object (133) You are Now Equipped to Change Your Life with Tele-Psychometry (133)

Chapter Seven— Miracle Healing Through Psychic Medi-Telemetry (135)

How Bertha P. Cured Her Husband of Alcoholism (135) How Ida Cured Her Mother's Senility (136) The Porcelain Cup Power Ritual (137) How Harvey C.'s Asthma Was Cured (138) Paul P.'s Epilepsy Miraculously Disappeared (139) The Gemstone Power Ritual (139) Gem Healing is Inexpensive (142) Color is Power (142) Evelina G.'s Miraculous Recovery (143) Harold F. Saw His Lung Change from Disease to Perfection (144) Ritual to Perform Healing By Color (144) The Power of Magnetic Healing (145) Audrey R.'s Spastic Colon Cured (147) Power Ritual for Magnetic Healing (147) Jack T.'s Eyesight Returned After Receiving Healing from a Guardian Genie (148) Your Healing Genie is Ready (148) Power Ritual to Perform Guardian Genie Healing (149) Distance is No Obstacle to the Psychic Telemetry Healing (149) Power Ritual to Perform Healings at a Distance (150) There are Some People Who Cannot Be Healed (150) Why an Illness Returns (150) Power Ritual for Diagnosing the Origin of a Disease (151) Thoughts Can Cause an Illness (151)

Chapter Eight — How to Use Psychic Astral-Telemetry for Getting Anywhere or Reaching Anybody (153)

In the Words of St. Paul, If There is Such a Thing as an Animal Body, There is Also a Spiritual Body" (153) How You Will Feel as Your Two Bodies Separate (154) Astral-Telemetry Experiences are Not Uncommon (155) How Astral-Telemetry Moved Reverend E. from a Storefront Church to a $125,000 Sanctuary

How to Use Psychic Astral-Telemetry for Getting Anywhere or Reaching Anybody (con't)

(156) How to Influence the Thoughts of Others Through Astral-Telemetry (159) How Rose K. Won a Legal Action Worth Almost $30,000 When She Learned That a Man Had Intentionally Killed Her Pet Dog (159) Astral-Telemetry is Harmless (162) How Delbert L. Passed a Vital Civil Service Examination by Using Astral-Telemetry (163) How to Use Astral-Telemetry to Accomplish an Out-of-the-Body Experience (164) How Tony R. Traveled Invisibly from Guam to San Diego and Proved that His Wife was Deceiving Him (165) How You Will Feel During Your First Astral Journey (166) How Harriet O. Performed an Astral Ritual to Gain the Love of a Man (167) You Can Now Go Anywhere and Reach Anybody (168)

Chapter Nine — Psychic Telemetry Games That Will Make You a Winner Every Time (171)

How Psychic Game One Revealed That Claudia F.'s Husband was Unfaithful (172) How Claudia F. Used Psychic Game One to Win Back Her Husband and Make His Temptress Beg for Forgiveness (173) How to Play Psychic Game One (175) The Psychic Game One Power Ritual That Wins Unfailing Control Over Others (177) Your Psychic Marble Can Make a Flower Grow (179) Psychic Party Games that Show You the Past, Present, and Future (179) Psychic Game Two (180) How Ivan D. Played Psychic Game Two and Found the Water that Saved His Vineyard (181) How Leona M. Used Psychic Game Three to Win a Vacation in Hawaii (183) How to Play Psychic Game Three (184) The Psychic Game Three Ritual (185) Additional Psychic Exercises that are Guaranteed to Make You a Winner Every Time (185) Psychic Exercise One Will Increase Your Powers of Sensory-Telemetry (186) Psychic Exercise Two Will Increase Your Powers of Visual-Telemetry (187)

Chapter Ten — Advanced Secrets of Psychic Telemetry For a Great New Life of Abundance, Health and Joy (189)

How Eleanor W. Used Her Combined Psychic Telemetry Powers to Become a Healthy, Desirable Woman and Won the Man She Loved (190) You Can Combine Your Psychic Powers to Perform a Miracle (192) The Advanced Psychic Telemetry Power Ritual (192) How to Increase Your Telemetric Sign Language with the Magic Rectangles (194) Color Your World with Psychic Power (196) How Wilfred B. Used Color to Sweep the Girls Off Their

Advanced Secrets of Psychic Telemetry For a Great New Life of Abundance, Health and Joy (con't)

Feet (197) How Francine E. Used Color to Save Her Marriage While It Healed Her Body (198) If There's An Evil Influence Lurking About You, Salt It Away (199) How Josephine L. Used Salt to Counterattack Her Evil Entities and Won (200) No Harm Will Come to You If You Make Unintentional Errors in Performing Your Psychic Telemetry Rituals, Enchantments, or Advanced Techniques (201) How to Use the Psychic Telemetry Trinity, Sand-Sulphur-Salt (202) Sand, Sulphur, and Salt Represent Air, Fire, and Water (202) How Ariel B. Used Sand, Sulphur, and Salt to Make Powerful Talismans for the Protection of Her Family (203) How to Make Your Own Cosmic Dust (204) How to Use Cosmic Dust as an Advanced Psychic Telemetry Technique (205) Gene H. Sprinkled Cosmic Dust at the Door of the Man Who Cheated Him. The Building Burned Down (206) Strike It Rich with Your New Psychic Telemetry Powers (207)

Psychic Telemetry:
New Key to
Health, Wealth and Perfect Living

Chapter One

Psychic Telemetry Has Reaped Miracles for Others— Just as It Can for You

Life appears to be so very complicated. It often seems that your entire existence is one of overcoming obstacles. You overcome one obstacle and, sure enough, there's another one to conquer.

Indeed, you spend so much time fighting the fires that continually appear in your life that you have little time available to devote to realizing the *real you*—the real you that pleads for health, fame, achievement, wealth, and love. But this need not continue, and it shouldn't continue.

Right now, at this very moment, *you* have the power to change your life from one of poverty to riches, to change a lonely life to one of love. Any of these things can be yours—and they will be yours before you have completed the last chapter of this book. *Psychic Telemetry* has been written especially for *you*, and I sincerely believe that you will find it to be the most important book that you have ever read. Look at this natural occurence:

"Bob, I had to tell you what happened to me," a voice on the telephone blurted out. "I was driving to Las Vegas. I was just going over a rise in the road when I heard a voice scream, 'Stop the car'! I applied the brakes as quickly as possible, and finally came to a stop just as I went over the crest of the hill. My God! It was terrible! A semidiesel truck had overturned, blocking the road. There were a dozen cars piled up in the accident. There was no way that I could have avoided hitting the cars strewn all over the highway. That voice saved my life."

This is a very simple example of helpful *Psychic Telemetry*. As the chapters of this book unfold, you will explore a hundred practical methods of harnessing this great realm of the unknown. But is this psychic realm really so unknown to you?

YOU HAVE ALREADY EXPERIENCED SIMPLE PSYCHIC TELEMETRY

Ever had a hunch? Did you ever experience "woman's intuition?" Did you ever sense someone staring at the back of your head? Where did your last idea come from? These are all expressions of the Great Cosmic Mind. The same Cosmic Mind that gave you your hunch, or a novel idea, is the same Cosmic Mind that gave struggling inventors the inspiration that has led to brilliant inventions which have revolutionized the world.

The Cosmic Mind has taken a penniless drifter and made him a millionaire, and raised the crippled and afflicted from their beds so that they might walk. These are not miracles. They are simple expressions of the power of *Psychic Telemetry*.

You possess these same powers of *Psychic Telemetry* at this very moment. Then why aren't you performing miracles? Simply because you have not learned how to use these miraculous powers that are standing quietly at your side—ready to go into action at a moment's notice. In reality, a "miracle a day" is nothing unusual, as you will soon discover for yourself.

THE GREAT MYSTICS VANISHED, BUT THEIR POWERS SURVIVE

Psychic Telemetry is not new. Its knowledge is old and was practiced for thousands of years in the ancient past.

The Mystics of old used their powers to heal the sick and enrich the poor. They brought hope, they even brought food and gold to the starving masses. They could bring rain to the drought-plagued crops. They brought lovemates to their friends and to their families.

Legend now portrays these Mystics as "gods," where in reality they were ordinary men and women, just like you. They merely had the knowledge to perform effortless miracles at any time of their choosing—and they performed thousands of miracles.

The Mystics jealously guarded their secrets lest the kings, princes, and potentates of their day discover the mystic power to use for further degrading mankind to an eternal state of serfdom and slavery.

As the Middle Ages dawned upon the horizon of mankind's evolution, the Mystic resisted the political and religious persecution that befell him. Some Mystics used their magical powers to transport themselves to other countries of the earth, where a semblance of these Ancient Teachings still survive.

Other Mystics chose the life of the hermit, withdrawing alone to caves and mountain tops where they could find peace to practice their magical powers. Occasionally, a weary stranger would stumble into the Mystic's camp to learn the magical powers of the Masters. These disciples would sometimes remain with the Holy Hermits for a century or more, performing their good for mankind, but never rejoining it.

There were other Mystics during the dark time of the Middle Ages who chose not to flee, but to remain among the poor and sick whom they had learned to love.

Withstanding torture, and dying upon the racks, these Wise Men died bravely, refusing to reveal their magical secrets to the rulers who would use the powers for evil instead of good.

Though the great Mystics were now dead, bits and pieces of their knowledge survived. Sorcerers, witches and alchemists stumbled upon portions of the Ancient Wisdom, and with these small bits of knowledge were able to perform wonderous feats. But their attempts at duplicating the miracles of the ancient Mystics were amateurish in comparison to the remarkable achievements of their predecessors.

Many of the Ancient Teachings were lost through the trial-and-error methods of the sorcerer and witch. They introduced ridiculous special effects, ranging from the wearing of black robes to howling at the moon like a forlorn coyote on the prairie.

Of all the special psychic and occult tools introduced over the centuries, none were successful in turning on the magical powers of the ancient Mystics. The real Key to Power escaped their grasp. The key that they could not find was the shattering power of the mind. With the power of the mind, *you* can now perform the miracles of ages past, using as your psychic tools, the same secret Pillars of Power that were known only to the last of the great Mystics who were executed during the Middle Ages.

It is my honest belief that no book before <u>*Psychic Telemetry,*</u> which you now hold in your hand, has ever revealed the total secrets held within the Pillars of Power.

THE PILLARS OF POWER HAVE NOW BEEN REDISCOVERED

The half-successful magical efforts of the more recent wizards, sorcerers, witches, psychics, etc., is because they have discovered only half of the magical power that is required before real miracles can be performed.

The magical key to the Pillars of Power is so obvious that possibly it was overlooked by the wizards because of its simplicity. They searched far and wide. Many traveled around the world to discover the secrets that are about to be revealed to you.

Searching, delving and studying, they looked so hard for the magical secrets, that they neglected to realize that they already had one of the Pillars of Power at their fingertips. They only needed to use the power of their own mind and make it explode into action.

INTUITION—YOUR PSYCHIC
LEGACY FROM AGES PAST

The first great Pillar of Power? Your intuition, or instinct.

The Great Cosmic Mind determined that man, at his creation, would possess the power of a god—the power to subvert all things to his will.

Man was not created and then left to drift and fend for himself, as best he could. If that had been the case, man would have immediately been destroyed by the hostile forces of nature that surrounded him on every side. A powerful force for self-protection and for the performing of miracles was, and is, given to every man and woman born on this planet.

A quick glimpse back to the primitive existence of the newly created earth reveals to us the animal whose only means of survival was reliance upon the instinct given it by the Cosmic Mind. The ancient animal knew when to migrate to warmer climes as the changing seasons approached. The animal could, by instinct, find water for its survival. It could sense approaching danger. This vital instinct was necessary for its survival in what was a dangerous and troubled world. And man was not neglected in this great scheme of creation.

In the evolutionary cycle of creation, prehistoric man was not gifted with a level of intelligence that could insure his survival through logical and deductive reasoning. Man could develop the power of the intellect through his own resources, but the power of intuition could only be given by the Creator.

Ancient man did develop his intellect, and as his intellect increased, he relied less and less upon his instinct for survival.

Man first used the club, then the ax, the bow, and the rifle as a means of protection and for tools to be used in the gathering of food. As these means of self-protection became more sophisticated, he erroneously believed that he no longer required reliance upon instinct. Ultimately, a conflict arose between man's rational mind and his instinctive mind. In haste, he chose to accept as complete reality only those things that he could touch, taste, see, etc. He chose to ignore those things which could be instinctively *sensed*.

Our forebears chose not to use their intuitive power, but it was by no means lost. The great Power of Intuition could not be lost or destroyed by our ancestors because it is the automatic birthright of every man and woman. It is *your* birthright! Intuition lies bubbling below the surface of your subconscious mind, ready to burst into action. And I am going to show you how to unleash this First Pillar of Power. The miracles that you can and will perform will leave you awe-struck.

HOW TO UNLOCK THE MIGHTY FORCE OF YOUR FIRST PILLAR OF POWER

The first step toward unlocking the force of your First Pillar of Power is to become as relaxed as possible. It is your choice whether this brief method of relaxation should be in a standing, sitting, or prone position. Now that you are relaxed in a comfortable position, close your eyes tightly. With eyes closed, visualize a flaming pillar of light in front of you and to the right. Watch this Pillar closely. It is your First Pillar of Power.

Now, repeat this positive Declaration:

"I am now relaxed and my eyes have shut out the cares of the world."

"I now command that my subconscious mind be activiated. My subconscious mind now opens to me and reveals its magical secrets."

Remain relaxed! You will be pleasantly surprised at the wonders that will now pour into your conscious mind.

ALEX R. CLUNG TO A WORTHLESS PARCEL OF TEXAS PRAIRIE—OIL WAS DISCOVERED!

This true case history was brought to my attention as I sat writing the pages of this chapter.

A few years ago Alex R. and his family owned worthless prairie land in southern Texas. The family was very, very poor. Though they owned hundreds of acres of land, they could neither afford the equipment necessary to farm the land, nor could they purchase cattle to graze upon it. The family fortune declined even further. It was necessary to put the land up for sale. But let Alex tell his own story.

"I remember, at the time all of this happened, I didn't know anything about the Pillars of Power or *Psychic Telemetry*.

"Anyway, we had reached the point that my family only had a few garden vegetables to eat. And these were eaten at our one meal a day. The smaller children had become lazy and listless from the very poor diet which we barely managed to survive upon. Dad decided that he had to sell our land and move the family into town.

"A large cattle rancher, whose land bordered ours, made Dad a fair offer on the property, and Dad decided to accept the offer.

"When the day arrived to sign the final papers of the sale, I awoke with a *feeling* that I had never experienced before. I *knew* that we had to hang onto the land, but I didn't know why.

"My pleas to my father fell upon deaf ears. 'In the first place, there is no way we can afford to keep the land,' he told me. 'In the second place, I think your *instinct* is crazy.'

"I begged, argued, and pleaded that we keep the land. I became so distraught in my urgings, that my father finally agreed to deed 40 acres to me, on one condition. The condition was that I must go to work at a full-time job to pay for the land. Getting a job at 16 wasn't easy, and it took nine years to pay for that land.

"During those nine years, I still had no idea as to why I had to keep that land. I kept telling myself that I was a darned fool, but even thinking of selling the land caused deep shudders. My *instinct* would tell me over and over again to 'hang on!'

"A couple of years ago, I became interested in *Psychic Telemetry,* and decided to perform the Ritual of the First Pillar of Power.

"I followed the instructions of the Ritual, and as soon as I had said its last word I heard a voice. The voice thundered, 'There's oil on your land!' Now I finally knew that all my years of struggling to keep that sagebrush-covered land was for a specific reason.

"I contacted an oil company, and after receiving the geological reports, the company agreed to sink a test well. Last week, the well came in.

"I'm rich! I have just received a check for $50,000, and that's just the beginning. I'll receive money from every barrel of oil produced from that well."

Alex R. concluded his letter by saying that he only wished he had heard of *Psychic Telemetry* years before. He was grateful that his *intuition* influenced him to keep his 40 acres. He could have been a millionaire years before if he had only known how to unlock his subconscious mind.

YOU CAN DO WHAT ALEX DID —AND FAR MORE

Alex's story is unique only because oil was discovered on his land. Hundreds of thousands of people every day receive the same instinctive urgings as those that alerted Alex to the good fortune at his fingertips. Unfortunately, few people heed their hunches as Alex did. Even fewer know how to use the Pillar of Power to unlock the subconscious mind. This is the essential ingredient needed to perform miracles, and to get rich quick! This is the ingredient that has been missed by modern Mystics.

Instinct is only one of the many aspects of *Psychic Telemetry* power. Imagine what you will be able to do when you have learned deeper and greater secrets of *Psychic Telemetry*. Remember, Alex only held one secret of *Psychic Telemetry* power. Yet, he worked himself a miracle.

I'm not exaggerating when I say the sky is the limit. You'll be able to alter any situation to suit yourself. You'll be an instant miracle worker!

THE SUBCONSCIOUS MIND IS THE COSMIC MIND

I do not want to become overly technical about how *Psychic Telemetry* works. *Psychic Telemetry* works just as efficiently for the person who knows nothing of its cosmic mechanics as for the person who is expert in the technical aspects of this awe-inspiring power.

Spiritually, man can never be separated from the Spirit which caused his creation. The vital link that keeps man in tune with the Infinite is the subconscious mind. It is this subconscious mind that is, in reality, the great Cosmic Mind. It knows all, and it tells all. It tells all to you as you unlock its mighty secrets through the Ritual of the First Pillar of Power.

HOW YOUR COSMIC MIND SPEAKS TO YOU

In later chapters you will learn that everything within the universe emits a vibration. You will learn how to use these vibrations to remove an evil spell, bring good luck, etc. It is these vibrations which speak to your Cosmic Mind.

Each person possesses five *psychic* senses that are exact, etheric duplicates of their five physical senses. It is these *psychic* senses that are aware of the vibrations that remain invisible to us. These etheric senses are stimulated by the unseen vibrations, and the information is transmitted to your subconscious mind where it is stored, until called upon by the First Pillar of Power Ritual, to reveal its secrets to your conscious mind. The expressions of the subconscious cause you to hear voices and sounds, to see clairvoyant pictures, and to feel, taste, and smell.

These sensory experiences are expressions of the Sensory, Audio, and Visual-Telemetry that you will be learning in the chapters which follow. Once you've discovered the secret, it's very simple.

THIS PSYCHIC POWER IS NOT DETERMINED BY AGE, SEX, OR RELIGION

Many people mistakenly believe that this awesome psychic power may, in some way, be governed by a person's sex, religion, or age. Nothing can be further from the truth.

Instinct is given at birth, to both male and female. This instinctive power is then carried within for the remainder of their life. Any religion that they might become involved in as they grow older has no influence upon their psychic power.

The age at which a person discovers the secret of opening the subconscious mind does not diminish or increase its power. No one is ever too old to perform miracles, nor are they too young.

The particular sex of an individual does not determine the extent of their psychic power. Society recognizes "woman's intuition," and would infer that intuition is the sole property of woman, but this is not the case. Men, through habit, do not refer to "man's intuition," but rather to "hunches." Hunches or intuition. It makes no difference what word you use. They all mean the same thing—*instinct!*

In writing this book, I use the word "man" quite frequently, but my usage of the word does not mean *a* man—it is used to denote *mankind,* as a race of beings, which includes both men and women.

HOW ALLEN F. WON $800 AT THE CRAP TABLE AFTER USING THE PILLAR OF POWER MAGIC RITUAL

Allen F. was the assistant pastor at a small and struggling church that faced eviction from its rented quarters. Things looked hopeless! It was Friday, and $800 was needed by Monday morning.

Psychic Telemetry Has Reaped Miracles for Others

Allen had never been inside of a gambling casino, and knew nothing about roulette, craps, or blackjack. He knew nothing about gambling, and had never been exposed to it, even in conversation.

I had known Allen for many years, and I was quite surprised when I received his telephone call. "Bob, I've got this crazy urge to go gambling at Reno. Will you go with me?" "Sure," I replied. Our party left the next morning. It was clear to me that Allen's instinct was trying to talk to him, and I wanted to witness the results.

When we arrived at Reno, it was obvious that Allen really didn't know anything about gambling. He had taken only 20 dollars. On this 20 dollars, he expected to eat three meals and still have plenty of money with which to gamble.

Allen was very surprised when in less than five minutes of gambling he had lost 19 of his 20 dollars. He looked dejected as he walked up to me.

"I only have one dollar left. I was sure that I was going to win the $800 that the church needed. Do you have a copy of that Ritual for the Pillar of Power?" I handed him a copy, and he stood reading it for a few moments. As Allen handed me back the pamphlet, I noticed that his eyes looked almost trancelike.

Allen silently turned, and it seemed as if he glided across the floor to a crap table. He had never before seen a crap table, and he certainly did not know how to play the game. I followed closely behind Allen and watched him intently. Without asking for instructions, Allen placed his lone silver dollar on the "Pass Line."

Allen threw the dice time after time, seven after seven. The table was mobbed with other players trying to get a piece of the action. The casino changed dice over and over again. There was no explanation for Allen's "hot streak" with the dice. "One more roll," Allen turned and said to me.

Allen counted his money as we walked from the table. He had won exactly $800—the 800 dollars needed to pay the back rent on his floundering church.

As we were driving away from Reno, I asked Allen where he had learned to shoot craps?

"I don't know how to play," he replied.

"If you don't know how to play, how could you stand there yelling, 'A dollar on the hard-way eight,' or 'I'll take odds on number six.' "

"Did I do that?," he asked.

Allen's innocence brought a roar of laughter from our party as we leisurely headed home.

Allen's church held a Thanksgiving Service on Monday evening, and I attended. Allen and I dropped our heads and smiled as Pastor Bartlett told his congregation, "God answers our prayers in strange and mysterious ways."

THE SECOND GREAT PILLAR OF POWER IS YOURS TO COMMAND

The second great Pillar of Power is all that remains between you and the secrets of the universe. And this secret power is now going to be revealed to *you*.

The First Pillar of Power taught you how to use the *inner*, instinctive power that you possess. The Second Pillar of Power will teach you to use those *outer* forces that will draw even more miraculous powers to do your every will.

THE GENIUS OF LONG GONE SOULS IS AT YOUR FINGERTIPS

There have been genuine instances where individuals have communed with the spirits of the dead, but there are limitations as to the help that these spirits can give. The mind within these spiritual beings is the same mind that they possessed on earth, and their knowledge is limited.

A lady with whom I was acquainted was communicating with her dead husband, who was giving her advice on financial investments. The lady lost everything. The last person she should have been asking advice from was her dead husband.

While alive on earth, John had gone through a literal fortune making bad investments, and his knowledge of wise money management did not increase with death, as the advice to his wife later proved.

Psychic Telemetry does not allow you to make these same errors. It teaches you to tap the Universal Mind, which is the source of infallible, good judgment.

The Universal Mind retains all knowledge of the past and present. It knows the course of future events, as the thoughts and knowledge of long gone earthly geniuses smolder within the Universal Memory. It is the accumulated knowledge of these souls from the past that will give you the power to become an instant miracle worker. There is no need to communicate with a very fallible individual spirit when you can rely upon the entire accumulated knowledge from human history. And this can be easily done by creating your own materialized thoughtform, or Guardian Genie.

HOW TO CREATE YOUR OWN GUARDIAN GENIE

You have no need of an individual Spirit Guide, but you do need to create a thoughtform which resembles the human form. This Guardian Genie, which you mentally create, will be a willing slave, ready to serve you for any purpose, at any time or any place.

WHERE TO BEGIN

Sit quietly with paper and pencil, jotting down each miracle you desire upon a separate page of paper. On these pages of paper, write a name. These will be the names of the Guardian Genie that you are about to create.

Also on these pieces of paper, write the physical characteristics that you want your Guardian Genii to possess. Black hair, blue eyes, tall, short, thin, or stout. Now, also list those abilities that each of your Guardian Genii will possess. Wisdom, power over others, humor, financial guidance, or healing power?

I remember very clearly the first Guardian Genie that I created. I was in junior high school, having difficulty with some of my studies. As I sat at my desk brooding, I decided to call upon the Genius Powers of Cosmic Mind to help me with my schoolwork. I took out a piece of paper and listed my requirements in a manner such as this:

**My Guardian Genie
For Schoolwork**

Name: Bennie
What Does He Look Like?: Bennie is a teenager with black hair and blue eyes. He is tall, thin, and knows the answers to all of my school problems.

As I grew older and matured, I created more and more Guardian Genii, each with a separate job to do. I created a thoughtform Spirit to give me advice on money, health, and love. They gave me all of these things, and your Spirit Geniuses will do the same things for you.

THE GUARDIAN GENIE CREATION RITUAL

After you have completed the creation of your Spirit Genius on paper, it is time to mold the thought force into a reality. Sit quietly, holding one sheet of paper before you at a time. Invoke this Power:

**"I am now in tune with the Infinite source of all knowledge and wisdom. This great Universal Mind will now identify itself to me in the form of a Guardian Genie, whose name will be_____.
____(name)____ will appear to me in this form: (Read aloud the physical characteristics of your Spirit Genius.) He or she will possess all knowledge needed to bring (your wish) into my life."**

Sit back and relax with eyes closed, visualizing the Spirit Genius you have just created. Follow this same Ritual for every Guardian Genie you wish to create. They never, never fail you.

HOW TO USE YOUR GUARDIAN GENIE
TO FULFILL YOUR EVERY COMMAND

Your Guardian Genii are powerful forces that stand ready to fulfill your every command. You have created a Genie to work miracles for you in health, wealth, happiness, etc. The more that you use these Genii, the more powerful they become.

Your Magic Genie should be called upon to work each time that you perform your Second Pillar of Power Ritual. When you perform this Ritual, call your Genie to you by name. Give him or her your command. You can be confident that they will work a miracle.

It would be repetitious if I were to remind you in each chapter of this book to call upon your Genie each time you perform your Second Pillar of Power Ritual. So, from this moment on, remember to call upon your appropriate Guardian Genie *each* time you perform your Second Pillar of Power Ritual.

LORRAINE T. PURCHASED THE DESERT LAND.
HER GUARDIAN GENIE FOUND THE WATER

Lorraine T. was a happy woman, but had very little in the way of material luxuries. She could never acquire enough money to buy a home or property. She held onto her dream, but had accepted her fate as an eternal apartment dweller.

It seemed a coincidence that the day after she read about a big land swindle in the daily newspaper, she received an advertisement from the same land development company that was under investigation. The company was accused of selling land that did not have water on it.

Natural curiosity led Lorraine to read the brochure. Rather than being repelled by the advertisement, Lorraine became intrigued. Her *instinct* was telling her to buy an acre of the worthless land, she later confided to her friends.

A heated battle between Lorraine's common sense and her instinct was taking place as she stood at the cashier's window, withdrawing the last dollar from her meager savings.

The deed to Lorraine's desert property was duly received. She opened the airmail envelope and stared at the worthless piece of paper. "What have I done?," she cried. Sinking into a deep state of mental depression, Lorraine swore that she would never reveal her stupidity to a soul.

Several weeks had passed before another coincidence occurred. While riding the bus home from work, Lorraine dropped a coin between the seat cushions. While reaching for the coin, she felt a piece of paper. After pulling up the wadded paper from the seat, she noticed that it was a small pamphlet entitled, "How to Create A Guardian Genie." With nothing better to do, Lorraine glanced through the paragraphs as she completed her bus ride home.

Lorraine was full of doubts as she performed *the Guardian Genie Creation Ritual* and, as she later said, "I was scared to death when I saw a form actually appear before me." But her fear was short-lived.

The well-driller did everything in his power to discourage Lorraine from wasting her money by having him drill for water. "The geologists said there isn't any water here," he said.

Armed with borrowed money and the guidance of her Guardian Genius, Lorraine walked onto her desert land and pointed to the spot where she wanted the well dug. The pipe was only drilled 24 feet when water was discovered! A miracle? No, just a wise and all-knowing Guardian Genius.

As you read further into *Psychic Telemetry*, you will discover that experiences such as this are common, everyday occurrences. Incidentally, Lorraine later sold her "worthless" desert property for enough money to purchase her dream house in southern California. And she was able to pay cash for her dream home.

RITUAL OF THE
SECOND PILLAR OF POWER

You have now given names to the Guardian Genii which you've created. These names and a quiet place to relax are all that is needed to invoke this next powerful Ritual.

Sit quietly upon a comfortable chair in a dimly lit room, feet flat upon the floor, hands resting, with palms up, on your knees. You are now ready to invoke the *Ritual of the Second Pillar of Power*.

With eyes closed, visualize your First Pillar of Power on your right. Then, with as much energy as possible, visualize your Second Pillar of Power in front of you, slightly to the *left*. When these two pillars of light are burning strongly, repeat the following words:

> "I now command that the Genius Mind, which lies within the Universal Intelligence, draw close to me now as I summon my Guardian Genie. __(name)__ will now appear to me.

Within seconds, the Spirit Genius will appear, standing directly in front of you between the two Pillars of Power. Make your desires known to the Genie and remain relaxed until he or she returns to tell you the information desired, or has completed the task assigned. The Ritual is completed when you repeat:

> "The Great Cosmic Mind has heard and answered my request. I give Thanks for my Genie and for my miracle."

PSYCHIC TELEMETRY ALWAYS HELPS— IT NEVER HARMS

These Pillars of Power Rituals show how *Psychic Telemetry* can work quietly and gently to change your life for the better. Yet these Powers are harmless to the user.

Whenever "magic" or "miracles" is heard, many people think of devils, demons, or evil spirits. Evil power is only a reflection of the confused attitudes of the Middle Ages. None of these ingredients is needed or used in *Psychic Telemetry*.

Chapter Two

Psychic Telemetry Enchantments That Automatically Bring You Floodtides of Cash, Treasure, and Security

You are now going to use genuine ancient magic to change the present and shape your future. Automatically and simply, whatever you ask for is about to become a reality.

These Enchantments are secret, and they are powerful. As you begin this exciting adventure into *Psychic Telemetry,* you should make absolutely certain that you have your desires clearly in mind. In that way, you will attune yourself with the mighty forces that will be exerted by your *Pillars of Power.*

The results of your Enchantments will be realized more quickly if you perform only one Enchantment a day. When you have fulfilled one desire, you can then use another Enchantment to bring your next wish into reality. So read this chapter carefully, for it will bring magical results to you within days, hours, or even minutes.

PSYCHIC TELEMETRY'S INITIATION RITUAL

This *Initiation Ritual* will be performed one time only. It will enroll you into the Ancient Society of Mystics. You will be at oneness with the ancient brotherhood of miracle workers who changed history as they performed their miraculous powers for themselves, and for others.

As you begin this very important Initiation Ritual, seat yourself and calmly perform the Ritual of your Pillars of Power. When both Pillars of Power are shining brightly, kneel before your chair with hands clasped, as if in prayer. Relax in this kneeling position for a few moments and invoke these sacred words of initiation:

"I ____(your name)____, now willingly enter the Ancient Society of Mystics. I am at oneness with the magical powers of the Cosmic Mind. I will perform all miracles with a sense of truth, justice, and selflessness. And so it is!"

Remain kneeling. You will feel an etheric hand placed upon your head as a sign of blessing, and as a sign of your acceptance into this Ancient Society of Mystics.

When this Ritual has been completed you will feel different. The difference you feel cannot be described by words, and I won't attempt to do so. This new feeling of power and vibrancy is your own special thing. Something special that is between the Cosmic Mind and yourself.

This Ritual is occasionally overpowering. You may feel weak or extremely emotional. If you do, don't be alarmed. Many people experience these new sensations of power in the same manner. Just lie down and relax for a few minutes. Your strength will soon return, and your feeling of emotion will soon be under control.

Psychic Telemetry Enchantments

Your greatest temptation will be from your exuberance at joining the Ancient Society. You will want to scream to the world of your happiness, but it's wiser to control your happiness and keep the new, powerful you a secret.

BE YOUR OWN SECRET SOCIETY

You will discover that most people will laugh and sneer at the power you are developing. They either disbelieve the power or they are frightened by it. In either case, these people will develop active mental opposition against your honest efforts to search for a new and better life. And it isn't opposition of conflict that you are looking for.

As you perform miracle after miracle, the day will soon dawn which makes it impossible for you to keep your secret. By that time you'll be rich, happy, and healthy. And then who cares? Let them laugh and ridicule to their hearts content. But until that time, remain a one-person secret society.

POWERFUL ENCHANTMENT FOR WINNING CONTESTS

"I command that Guardian Genie who brings good fortune to appear before me now.

"I command that my Pillars of Power remain strong and vibrant as I require my instinct and my Spirit Genius to influence the results of the contest I am about to enter.

"I have stated my desire and I command that it be fulfilled."

HOW AGNES C. WON OVER $500,000 WITH THE ENCHANTMENT FOR WINNING CONTESTS

Agnes C., from the eastern United States, would be the first to admit that she was an ordinary housewife from a family who just never had enough to make ends meet.

When Agnes attended a course of lectures on Enchantments, Spells, etc., she insisted that she possessed no psychic powers and never had a personal experience that she could consider as evidence of any latent psychic powers.

She found the lectures interesting, but made no effort to perform a miracle or use any Enchantments to enhance or improve her life.

A few weeks after the completion of the lectures, Agnes became sleepless because of a recurrent dream that awakened her night after night. The meaning of the dream was quite obvious, but it escaped Agnes' comprehension. She confided her dream to a friend.

> "Every night when I'm sleeping the soundest, a man wakes me up. He's dressed in flowing robes that are decorated with brilliant gold dollar signs.
> "The man then walks to the foot of my bed and holds seven fingers up in the air, all the time saying, 'A dollar a day keeps poverty away!'
> "The dream is driving me nuts!"

Agnes was so disturbed by her dream—not because it was frightening, but because she couldn't understand it—that her friend suggested a shopping excursion to get Agnes' mind away from the dream. While shopping, Agnes' friend said, "Let's stop here for a minute. There's only seven days left to buy tickets for the Lottery."

"Seven?" Agnes mused, "Could that be what my dream's been all about?" Agnes bought a lottery ticket, but didn't give the matter a great deal of thought. "The chances are one in a million that anyone could win any kind of prize from the drawing," she told her friend.

The subject of the coming lottery drawing came up in conversation at the supper table that evening. It was then that Agnes rummaged through her purse looking for the Enchantment to Win Contests. "I'm going to use that Enchantment and I'm going to win," she confidently declared.

Agnes performed her Enchantment one time daily for the next six days. And at the same time each day, she purchased a one-dollar lottery ticket.

Agnes and her entire family were on pins and needles as the day of the big drawing approached.

> "I was positive that I'd win something from the lottery, at least one of the smaller prizes. I simply could not believe it when my number was drawn for the grand prize. I won over a half-million dollars. I still can't believe it!"

Agnes and her family are now enjoying their new lakefront home with its private boathouse and dock. They have two expensive autos and all of the other luxuries that money can buy. "What a change has taken place in our life," she said. "An Enchantment lifted us from poverty to riches!"

HOW TO PERFORM YOUR ENCHANTMENT RITUAL

All of your Enchantment Rituals are slight variations from the Ritual of the Pillars of Power.

As you begin your Enchantment Ritual, know exactly what it is that you want to accomplish. There can't be any, "I think I want such and such." Be specific. There is no room for generalizations as you perform your magical and powerful Enchantments.

Sit in your dimly lit room, with your spine erect and hands resting upon your knees, palms up. Visualize your First Pillar of Power on your right, and declare:

> **"The First Pillar, which is the power of my instinct, will now vibrate with energy as I command it to fulfill the Enchantment that I now repeat."**

Repeat the Enchantment that will fulfill your desire. Remain seated, visualizing your Second Pillar of Power on the left. When the Pillar is strong and bright, repeat these magical words:

> "The Second Pillar, which is the Genius Intellect of the great Cosmic Mind, now hears and obeys my command. My Guardian Genie will now respond to my Enchantment and bring it into reality.

Repeat the same Enchantment used after the First Pillar of Power Ritual above. Now you can relax and wait. Your miracle is on its way. This exact Ritual should be performed for each Enchantment that you desire to exercise.

ENCHANTMENT FOR PERSONAL RECOGNITION

> "The strengthened Pillars of Power now respond and know that I require personal recognition for all of my talents and abilities.
> "I command that those people holding places of power and authority will now recognize all of my diligent efforts.
> "The Cosmic Powers now ordain that my wishes shall be fulfilled. The Pillars of Power will now, this very instant, have dominion over all forces that would keep me from my goal. I am the ruler of my destiny and have declared that Personal Recognition is now mine, forevermore. And so it is!"

HOW LARRY X. WENT FROM CLERK TO ENGINEERING SPECIALIST

Larry X. was a quiet man. He worked as a poorly paid clerk, with little opportunity for recognition or advancement. The computer company for whom he was employed was known for its opportunities for advancement, and the high wages it paid its employees. Yet, Larry remained at his same position. The wage increases he did receive were not sufficient to cover his spiralling cost-of-living increases.

Psychic Telemetry Enchantments

No one contested the fact that Larry's job performance was excellent. The reasons for skipping over Larry when it came to promotions remained a mystery to him and his fellow workers.

Larry was deeply in debt. He took care of his mother, and his wife required treatment by expensive medical specialists. He also had two daughters, and he was trying to financially help them through college. Without a promotion and more money, he would soon have to file for bankruptcy.

He talked with me on the telephone late one afternoon.

"Bob, I think my only problem is that I just sit and do my work," he said. "All the other guys do less work than I do, but they make a lot of noise about what they do, and everyone notices them. No one seems to know that I'm even around."

I asked Larry why he didn't make more noise so the bosses would notice him.

"I just can't do that," he replied. "It just isn't my nature to be loud and boisterous. A person should be recognized on his merits, not on what kind of a politician he is."

Larry was familiar with *Psychic Telemetry,* but he had never used any of its Enchantments. He wasn't sure that he even believed in such psychic things. It was from a feeling of desperation that he decided to try the Enchantment for Personal Recognition. He began his once-a-day Enchantment on Monday morning.

On Thursday, a severe problem was discovered in some new computer equipment. There was panic and chaos. The machine was to be shipped to the company's largest account. If it wasn't delivered as promised, hundreds of thousands of dollars in revenue would be lost.

Larry knew basic electronics, but could not be considered as any type of electronic engineer. The professional engineers kept running into stone walls. They could not find the origin of the problem.

At this point, Larry took the schematic drawings of the electronic marvel and poured over them. Then he opened the covers to the giant computer and peered inside. In his usual quiet manner, Larry called the company vice-president to his side.

"See the resistors, diodes, and capacitors in this area? Moisture is accumulating there and causing a magnetic obstruction as the electrical impulses attempt to pass."

At first, no one believed Larry, but later tests proved he was correct.

When Larry's diagnosis of the computer problem was confirmed, the vice-president gave him an unheard of, on-the-spot promotion. Larry's salary went from $220 a week to $300. And that wasn't the end of it. The following week, Larry's department was called for an impromptu meeting. He was presented with a $1500 check for his outstanding contribution in solving the computer dilemma.

The last word I heard from Larry was that he had received another in a line of many promotions. His salary had skyrocketed from $11,000 a year to almost $40,000.

"Believe me," he said, "I have no intention of staying where I am. The sky's the limit and I'm going after it."

If Larry uses his Enchantments properly, I have no doubt that he will continue to receive all of the success and personal recognition he desires.

PSYCHIC TELEMETRY ENCHANTMENTS WORK BEST WHEN USED FOR GOOD

You have probably already performed miracles with *Psychic Telemetry,* or are in the process of deciding just exactly what you want as you prepare to perform a miracle. *Psychic Telemetry* always works, but it produces more magnificently if your motives are just and honorable as you repeat these magical Enchantments.

Perform a miracle only when a miracle is required. If you want $1,000, don't ask for $20,000. Money is always available to you. You can get any amount of money at any time you need it. Just take what you need and leave the extra money for someone else to use until you require it for yourself.

Enchantments that are performed frivolously usually go unanswered. You must know exactly what it is that you want.

And then you must perform your Rituals and Enchantments with all due seriousness of purpose. General requests that are given in a light-hearted manner are answered in a like manner. Be specific in your requests, and be serious.

ENCHANTMENT FOR HEALTH

"I[1] bask in the sunlit energy of my Pillars of Power. The great rays of healing power now enfold me. They pulsate within every nerve and cell of my body; cleansing, soothing, and healing.

"I now command that all sickness and disease be banished from my mind and body. My perfect Spirit has now made me whole."

HOW LESTER W. CONQUERED HIS MIGRAINE HEADACHES BY USING THE ENCHANTMENT FOR HEALTH

Lester W., an accountant in Colorado, had suffered from headaches for as long as he could recall. Les was not the ordinary sufferer. He had three separate, but identifiable, head pains. Two types of headaches were cured by surgery, but Les continued to be plagued by very painful migraine headaches.

Before I met Les, he had had two operations to help alleviate his dreadful head pains. The first operation was on the sinuses. This relieved Les of one type of headache. The second operation required the severing of the occipital nerves in his head. This operation relieved him of the occipital neuralgia that had been causing him great pain.

Les was 54 years old when I first met him. His conversation was filled with the problems resulting from his severe migraine attacks.

"I have an attack about every ten days, and they last from 12 to 36 hours," he said. "The only thing I can do is go to bed until they pass."

---

[1] If you wish someone other than yourself to be healed, use his or her name instead of "I."

Les had suffered head pain for so long, that he was just about to give up all hope of ever being pain-free.

Les' employer had a very generous pension plan. Any employee who completed 30 years of service could retire at age 55. But Les lamented, "I've been missing so much work over these headaches, that I'm afraid I'm going to be fired before I'm 55."

Les began his Health Enchantment the first night I met him, and he never had another migraine attack. He happily retired at age 55, and began a three-month vacation touring the United States.

Finally free of his excruciating pain, Les felt years younger. In fact, he felt so good that he went back to work as an executive in another company.

"My health is perfect now. I just can't believe that this is really me! I didn't know what a beautiful world it really is," were the last words I heard from Les.

THIS MAGICAL ENCHANTMENT WILL GIVE YOU POWER OVER OTHERS

"I now send forth the mystic rays of my Pillars of Power to impress those whom I command to bend to my will at all times.

"I radiate power to dominate those who would oppose me. My Guardian Genie makes all who would block my wishes bend to my will. And so it is!"

HOW HAMMON D. WAS ELECTED COUNTY SUPERVISOR

Hammond D. is a supervisor of one of the fastest-growing counties in the United States. This county itself has a larger population than some American states.

I first met Hammon during a hotly contested election for county supervisor. All of the polls indicated that there was no chance that Hammon could wrest the supervisor's seat from the incumbent.

There were barely a dozen people present when I went to the neighborhood community center to listen to Hammon's election program. It was obvious that he was a fighter who had no selfish motives in proposing unique innovations to the operation of the county government. But it appeared from the low turnout of prospective voters that the polls were correct in predicting Hammon's defeat.

After the meeting, I handed him a leaflet containing the Enchantment to Influence Others. On the front of the leaflet I wrote, "Congratulations to our new county supervisor."

The news media was astounded as the election returns were posted. Hammon had unseated a supervisor who had not lost an election in 25 years.

A few days after the election, I received a hastily written note on new county stationery. It simply said, "Thanks!"

ENCHANTMENT THAT WILL LET YOU KNOW WHAT OTHERS ARE THINKING

"My mind is now open and clear.

"I Command that my Pillars of Power now inspire me to know the thoughts of __(name)__.

"My Guardian Genie now attends me.

"I can now hear, see, and sense what is in his or her mind.

"Whether awake or asleep, I will know these thoughts until I command that they cease. And so it is!"

HOW CINDY F. USED THE ENCHANTMENT TO KNOW WHAT OTHERS WERE THINKING TO EARN $500 A MONTH FROM HER HOBBY

Cindy F. was a happy homemaker dabbling in creative writing as a hobby. She had written hundreds of articles without selling even one of her creations. She came to expect the mimeographed rejection slips from prospective publishers. Though editors did take the time to tell her that her articles were good, they were just not on the subject matter that they were considering for publication.

Cindy had been given copies of *Psychic Telemetry* Enchantments, but had not felt the need to try them—at least not until she decided that she would try the Enchantment To Know What Others Are Thinking. "Maybe I can use this Enchantment to see what's in the mind of the editors—what type of article they are really looking for," she said.

Cindy chose the name of a professional magazine editor and performed her Pillars of Power Ritual, and her Enchantment. A thought flashed instantly through her mind! "The editor wants a confessional story with an occult slant to it!" Cindy thought that the idea was crazy, but decided to at least give it a try. She was pleasantly surprised when she received her first check for $75.00. She was even more surprised when the magazine editor wrote her a personal letter asking for more stories.

"I still had my doubts about the Enchantment," she later confided to me. "I thought that maybe it was a coincidence. As a test, I concentrated on another editor. I heard 'Write historical occult quizzes.' I wrote the quizzes and immediately sold them. That Enchantment really works!"

Cindy has acquired a good name in the magazine publishing business, selling every article that she writes. "I could sell a lot more articles," she recently told me on the telephone, "but I want to keep my writing just as a hobby. I just write enough articles to earn about $500 a month for extra spending money, then I stop for awhile to enjoy my success."

If Cindy can earn $500 a month from her hobby, just imagine for a moment what she could do if she wanted to turn her hobby into a career!

This Enchantment worked for Cindy, and the very same Enchantment will work for you.

ENCHANTMENT TO MAKE YOURSELF DESIRABLE

"I now declare that the Pillars of Power have made me attractive and desirable.

"My Guardian Genie will now guide my perfect partner to me. He or she will be blind to my shortcomings, whether they be physical or mental.

"My perfect partner will fulfill my every need and my every desire. And so it is!"

HOW ALBERT V. FOUND A PERFECT PARTNER

Albert V. was 45 years old and living in New Orleans when I first met him.

"The only reason I came to hear your lecture tonight is because it's free and I don't have anything else to do," Albert told me as he filed into the meeting room. Only during the part of the presentation where I explained the Power of Enchantments did Albert show any interest in the evening's lecture. He hesitated to leave after the meeting, obviously wanting to talk.

"Do you think those Enchantments would help me?," he asked. I assured him that they would.

Albert's problem was loneliness. "Two years ago my wife ran away with another man," he sadly related. "She left me with three children to raise, and it hasn't been easy."

"Why don't you remarry?," I asked

"Have you ever tried to find a woman who is willing to take on the burden of raising three small children? I sure as heck haven't found one."

Al found many women interested in him, and there were some who were very interested in marriage—at least until they discovered the three children who would become part of their marriage responsibilities.

"I need a wife, and my children need a mother. Will an Enchantment really help me?" he asked.

I saw Al a few months later—he was on his honeymoon in San Francisco.

"The Enchantment really worked," he said. "I repeated it for five days, once each day. On the sixth day, one of my children brought a note home from school. The note was inviting all parents to an 'open house' at the school.

"I attended the open house and met my daughter's teacher. It was love at first sight. The sparks really flew when our eyes first met. I just can't describe how she fussed over me. I was almost embarrassed over all of the attention she was giving me—but I loved it."

The best was yet to come. Albert knew he had found the perfect partner for himself, but what about a mother for his children?

"Everything is perfect. Ellie loves the children, and they adore her. No more loneliness for me. Thanks a lot!"

There was no need to thank me. It was a *Psychic Telemetry* Enchantment that deserved his gratitude.

GENERAL ENCHANTMENT FOR PROSPERITY

If you have no particular dollar figure in mind, nor a particular place from where *you* want to receive your new prosperity, then this Enchantment is for you! Repeat these words three times (once in the morning, once at midday, and once before retiring for the evening):

**"My Guardian Genie hears me now.
"Everything and everybody prospers me NOW!"**

HOW DEREK J. WENT FROM WISHFUL THINKER TO COMPANY PRESIDENT

Derek J.'s business was radio production. His business was in a state of great uncertainty, and it seemed impossible that he

Psychic Telemetry Enchantments

could meet his ever-mounting debts. And there was no new business in sight.

"I had heard of the Prosperity Enchantment, but hadn't thought to use it. I was on the subway, on my way to work, when I remembered the Enchantment and began repeating it over and over.

"The next day, I was *led* to call an acquaintance in the financial world whom I hadn't seen in over a year. When I called him, he wanted to see me immediately. We had lunch and I laid out my business plans before him. He immediately agreed to give me the loan I needed, but he insisted that the loan be interest free.

"I am now signing stock certificates as president of my new company."

I don't know how much money Derek is now worth, but a respected financial publication reported that the first year's profits from his new company were in six figures—over $100,000.

MARY D. NEEDED $400. SHE PERFORMED HER ENCHANTMENT AND HAD THE MONEY IN 45 MINUTES

Mary D.'s is a simple story about the power of *Psychic Telemetry* Enchantments.

Mary's car had to be towed to the garage after stalling on the freeway. Mary was by no means rich, and became terribly upset when the mechanic said, "It'll take about $400 worth of repairs to get your car running again, lady." She left her car at the garage, but had no idea where she could get the needed money.

Mary needed some cheering up after her depressing news, and she just *felt* like she should stop by her sister's house. Mary's sister was really in tune with *Psychic Telemetry* Enchantments, and suggested that they repeat the Prosperity Enchantment together.

A mere 45 minutes after the sisters declared their Prosperity Enchantment, the telephone rang. The call was from a cousin living in Minnesota.

"I was just calling to tell you that we sold some old farm equipment off of Uncle Oscar's farm. As he doesn't have any children, he wants all of his nephews and nieces to enjoy the money. Your share is $400. I'll mail it to you today."

ENCHANTMENT TO INCREASE SELF-ESTEEM

There is no need to feel shy, withdrawn, afraid, or inferior. You have within you, at this very moment, everything that is required to make you a confident, outstanding person.

After performing your Ritual of the Pillars of Power each day, repeat these magic words:

"I am confident and secure in each thing that I do and say.

"My every action demonstrates my attunement with the great Cosmic Mind. I reflect this Divine Intelligence in every thought, word, and deed."

HOW "PLAIN JANE" BECAME A FASHION MODEL

Jane D. was a shy, middle-aged housewife. She felt her life had been rather dull and unrewarding. Jane had many desires, but felt completely inadequate to follow any of them to a successful conclusion. All of her wishes required that she would have to be active before the public, and her shyness prevented her from any attempt to achieve her goals. "I could never get up before an audience," she often said.

A kindly neighbor suggested that Jane use the Enchantment To Increase Personal Esteem. "The effort will be worthwhile even if it only helps you to carry on a conversation in a crowd," she told Jane. "It's no fun being a wallflower while everyone else is always having so much fun."

Jane started the Enchantment on a Thursday. Almost immediately, she *felt* a new sense of poise and sophistication within her. She was sensitive to how she walked and talked. She was elated to discover that she could look a person right in the eye as she spoke to them—no longer lowering her own eyes from timidity.

During a shopping excursion the week after her Enchantment began, she stumbled upon a fashion show already in progress at the city's largest department store.

Jane was not embarrassed, or offended, as she noticed a man staring at her intently. For the first time in her life she actually felt flattered. She wasn't at all surprised when the male admirer approached her after the show.

"Are you a model?" he asked.

"No, just a housewife."

Those two sentences were the beginning of Jane's modeling career.

The gentleman who approached Jane was the designer of the clothes that had just been shown. He was so impressed by Jane's sophisticated and regal bearing, that he hired her on-the-spot to model the formal evening wear at all future fashion shows.

"Plain Jane" now loves the spotlight and the glamour. "And besides," she says, "$35 an hour isn't a bad wage."

ENCHANTMENT FOR PROTECTION FROM EVIL

"I am now in attunement with the pure rays of power that come to me from the Great Cosmic Mind.

"My Guardian Genie stands ready to protect me from every curse or evil influence.

"I am surrounded with divine protection, and no evil can penetrate my shield of power.

"Those who would send me evil are powerless, and their evil shall return to them a hundredfold."

HOW THE ENCHANTMENT AGAINST EVIL TURNED THE TABLES ON SALLY'S TORMENTOR

Sally was an attractive secretary in the home office of a large insurance firm when she wrote to me:

"All of the fellows in the office have made good-natured passes at me, and there were never any hard feelings when I rejected their advances until a new man transferred into the office—and he scares me to death.

"He's all honey and sweetness when anyone is around, but as soon as he's sure he can't be overheard, he tells me that he hates me and has put a curse on me.

"The telephone rings all night. And when I answer the phone no one is there.

"Now my landlord has asked me to move. He says he has heard from a good authority that I'm not the type of woman whom he wants in his apartment building.

"Can't you please do something to help me get rid of this evil man? He's driving me toward a nervous breakdown."

I wrote to her and enclosed the Enchantment for Protection From Evil. I told her to perform the Ritual daily until the evil was removed from her life.

Two weeks later, I heard from Sally again.

"I felt a lot better after I performed my Ritual for the first time. I wasn't as afraid as before. I didn't even dread getting up and going to the office. I just *knew* inside that in some way my tormentor was going to be taken care of.

"I had been saying the Enchantment for seven days when that man came up to my desk. He leaned toward me and whispered all kinds of obscene remarks. But this time, another fellow in the office overheard him. Right then and there, my tormentor was given a real beating by the man who overheard his remarks.

"When the big boss came from his office to find out what the ruckus was about, he fired that evil man, and I haven't seen or heard from him since."

ENCHANTMENTS WORK EXCITING MIRACLES

Enchantment miracles are so exciting, that many people find it difficult to remain serene and peaceful as they work their magic spells. Miracles are truly exciting events, but with practice you'll soon discover that you do indeed remain in a state of aloof calmness as the Cosmic Mind, your Pillars of Power, and your Guardian Genie fulfill your every wish and desire.

Chapter Three

How Visual-Telemetry Will Give You the Magnetic King Midas Golden Gaze

You are already well-equipped to change the future by using the Enchantments and the Ritual of the Pillars of Power from the preceding chapters. But *seeing* into the future is what this chapter is all about.

There is no need to blindly stumble into the future when you now have the tool to *see* any future obstacle before you. When you can clearly see an obstacle, you can take the corrective action needed to avoid it.

**GARY U.'S KING MIDAS GOLD GAZE MADE HIM
ONE OF AMERICA'S NEWEST MILLIONAIRES!**

Gary U. was so down on himself, that he seriously considered suicide. Due to his overextravagence, the bills mounted and mounted. The more the bills piled up, the more he became miserable and unhappy. No longer able to bear Gary's outbursts of temper, his wife left him and moved to Los Angeles.

Gary had started each evening with a drink to calm his nerves. Before long, the evening drink wasn't enough. Gary nipped at a bottle of whiskey before, during, and after his working hours. He was consuming a full bottle of whiskey daily when his employer reluctantly fired him for being drunk on the job.

Luckily for Gary, a fellow worker was familiar with Visual-Telemetry, and was willing to take the time to explain to Gary that he shouldn't despair. "I'll teach you to look into the future. You'll see that you have a lot to live for," Gary's friend told him.

"I don't believe a bit of that baloney," Gary replied.

It took a great deal of persuasion before Gary agreed to stay sober long enough to at least try the Visual-Telemetry Ritual. Though he agreed to try the Visual-Telemetry Ritual while sober, Gary just didn't get around to it for quite awhile. His condition continued to deteriorate until he awoke from a drunken stupor to find himself in a skid row flophouse. Gary was horrified as he peered through bloodshot eyes at the physical and mental derilects lying upon the dirty flophouse mattresses. He rose quickly and fled to a nearby park.

As his brain cleared, Gary determined that he had to change his pattern of living. But what could he do? What did the future really hold for him?

"I sat on a park bench just looking around. There were flowers, and there were children with their families. I didn't have any of these things." Then Gary began to look inward.

> "I could remember clearly the Ritual for Visual-Telemetry. I decided it was the only thing that could hold any glimmer of hope. I did a few visualization exercises and performed the Ritual. I could not believe the pictures that flooded into my mind. I wondered if I was really seeing into the future, or if I had a very vivid imagination."

What Gary saw within his mind were simple pictures, but they were the most important pictures of his life.

"The first thing I saw within my mind was a picture of my wife. She was waving her right hand. And in her hand I saw a check for $6,000. This seemed impossible. But the more I thought about the vision, the more anxious I became to telephone her. As I placed the telephone call, I had strong doubts that she would even accept my collect call.

"Maureen did accept my call, and the rest is history."

What happened when Gary placed the call to his wife isn't a mystery to a *Psychic Telemetry* follower. After talking to Maureen, Gary learned that an attorney had been trying to contact him. A long-forgotten cousin had died and left Gary $6,000 in her will. All Gary had to do was claim the money in person and sign the proper papers. Gary immediately started hitch-hiking toward Los Angeles.

While riding south with a friendly truck driver, Gary "tuned in" to his Visual-Telemetry. He was surprised to see a picture of himself in a stockbroker's office, purchasing shares in a company he had never heard of. At the next truck stop, Gary looked in the financial section of the daily newspaper. Sure enough, he found the company which he saw in his vision listed on the New York Stock Exchange.

Gary was waiting at the attorney's door the next morning. He knew what he was going to do. As soon as he received his check, he was going to buy stock. Stock in a company that he knew nothing about. Gary received his money and dashed to the nearest stockbroker.

The stockbroker was a considerate man who tried hard to dissuade Gary from buying the manufacturing stock. "That company is on the verge of bankruptcy. Don't waste your money on that stock," he said. However, at Gary's insistence, the stock was purchased at $3.00 per share. Gary had almost 2,000 shares of what many considered to be worthless stock. But Gary hung on. In just a few months, Gary's stock was worth almost $66,000.

Gary knew from a previous Visual-Telemetry vision that he should sell his manufacturing stock when it reached $33 per share. He was to sell this stock, then purchase stock in a computer company. Gary's vision was correct. The computer stock rose dramatically, and Gary sold his shares for over $118,000.

With money worries far behind, Gary and his wife reconciled and have never been happier. Gary so impressed the brokerage firm with his ability to make money while so many others failed, that he was employed as a financial consultant to the firm.

I have recently read in a financial review that Gary is one of America's newest millionaires. And all because of Visual-Telemetry's King Midas Golden Gaze.

VISUAL-TELEMETRY—
A LOOK INTO THE FUTURE

Visual-Telemetry is the ability to see pictures relating to the future without reliance upon the physical eyes. These *visions* of the future are seen *within* the mind, and are as real as any image you have ever seen with your physical eyes wide open.

Before you perform the simple Visual-Telemetry Ritual that I will shortly reveal to you, perform these three visualization exercises:

Here is a drawing of a simple flower. Look at it for just a few moments.

You can see the flower very well with your physical eyes. But now, close your eyes and visualize the flower within your mind. Open your eyes and look at the flower. Then, close your eyes and look at the same flower within your mind.

The vision of the flower that you see within your mind is Visual-Telemetry. Your visions of the future will appear in your mind with the same force as the image of the flower in this exercise.

Visual-Telemetry

Here is another simple drawing. Practice seeing the image first with your physical eyes, and then with your "psychic eyes."

Now that you have fully visualized the tree, move on to this next drawing which is a bit more complicated.

Exercises such as this are not necessary for successful Visual-Telemetry. I give them only as simple aids to assist you in recognizing the Visual-Telemetry visions that will very shortly be bombarding your conscious mind with all types of glimpses into the future. You'll soon be receiving more visions of the future than the famous psychics and seers you read so much about in your magazines and newspapers.

By performing three simple exercises, you have been initiated into the secrets of Visual-Telemetry. Now, the only ingredient you need before becoming a full-fledged prophet of the future is the performance of your Ritual of the Visions.

RITUAL OF THE VISIONS

Seat yourself in a dimly lit room and perform your Ritual of the First Pillar of Power.

Visual-Telemetry

When your First Pillar is alive and pulsating, visualize the Pillar enclosed in a large triangle. Each point of the triangle signifies one of the three powerful psychic abilities. The bottom point of the triangle represents Visual-Telemetry, the other two points signify mystic powers that you will learn in Chapter Four.

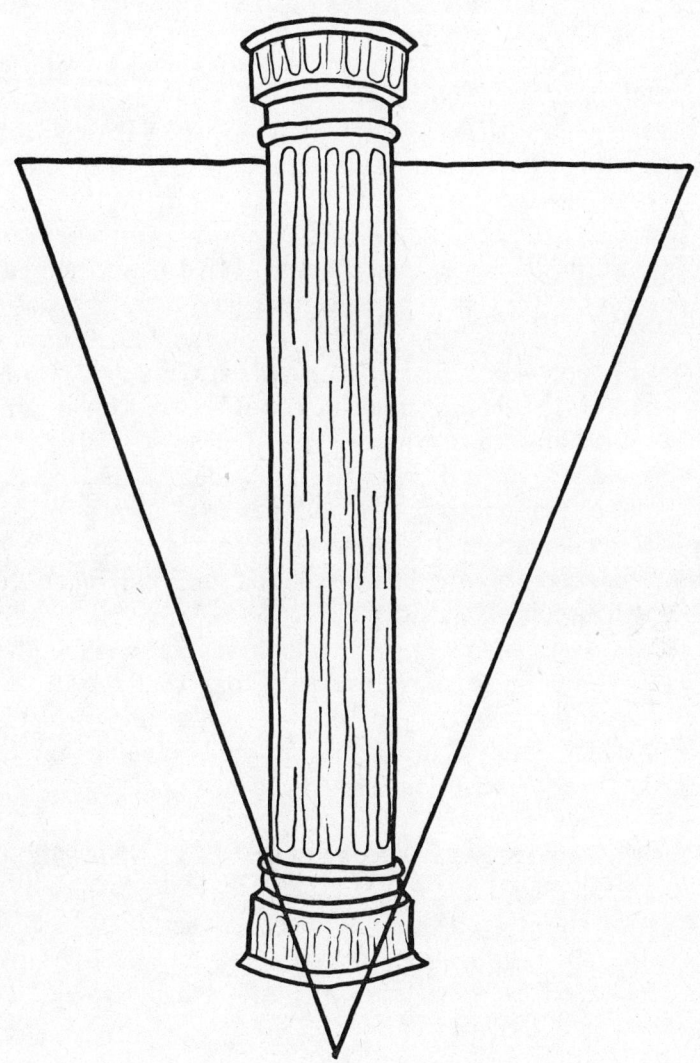

As you visualize the Pillar of Power and the Magic Tele-Triangle, repeat these words in a quiet, sing-song voice:

> "My psychic eyes have opened,
> And now I can see,
> All of the visions,
> That there are for me."

Now sit relaxed for a few moments. Vision upon vision will flash brilliantly into your mind.

At this point, perform your Second Pillar of Power Ritual, and ask your appropriate Guardian Genie to help give power to your Visual-Telemetry experiences.

If you have no specific request as you receive these visions from the future, allow the Great Cosmic Mind to sift and filter unimportant things from your visions of the future. The Cosmic Mind will present you with the visions of the future that are essential to your well-being. If there is danger ahead, Cosmic Mind will flash you the warning so a possible catastrophe can be avoided. If for any reason you are confused by your vision, ask your Guardian Genie to step in and clarify your psychic message.

If there is tremendously good news in the future, the Cosmic Mind can show it to you. And, if assistance is needed, you can then take the proper action to ensure that your future miracle will become a positive reality.

If you desire to receive a vision about a certain place, person, or thing, it is only necessary to verbally state your request. For example, if you wish to invest money in certain stocks or bonds that will bring you the greatest return on your investment, simply state:

> "I will now visualize the stocks and bonds that will make me rich," or
> "I will now receive a vision of the place where I can gain employment," or
> "I now receive a vision of my future marriage partner,"
> etc.

HOW DOROTHY K. RECOVERED AN $8,000 LOAN THAT SHE THOUGHT WAS LOST FOREVER

When Dorothy K. felt an instinctive nudging to have her fiancé sign a paper acknowledging her $8,000 loan to him, she listened.

"At the time I made the loan, I felt stupid asking my fiancé to sign a paper for the money—we were to be married in a few weeks," she later wrote to me. "But my intuition and my Guardian Genie demanded that I get a receipt for the money. And was I ever glad that I did!"

A few days prior to Dorothy's planned wedding, her fiancé told her that he had to return to his hometown on urgent business. When a week passed without any word, Dorothy traced him by telephone. Dorothy was shocked when a woman answered the telephone and idenified herself as the wife of the man Dorothy had fully expected to marry.

As the story unfolded, Dorothy found that her lover was not divorced as she had believed, but was only separated from his legal wife. Dorothy was heartsick, but consoled herself by thinking how lucky she was for not marrying that horrible man, as she originally planned. She was by no means rich, but looked at the $8,000 loan as a bad debt, with no hope of ever recovering it.

Two years later, Dorothy found herself out of a job and in dire need of every penny she could scrape up. She wrote to her ex-fiancé and asked that he repay the $8,000 loan, or at least a part of it. He refused to pay Dorothy, stating that he had no money, was self-employed, and did not earn a steady income. Her only recourse was to file a lawsuit to recover her money, but before the suit was brought against Marc, he filed for bankruptcy.

Dorothy had given up all hope of getting her money, until she sat down one evening to ask her Visual-Telemetry to show her a vision of how she would get the money to meet her mounting debts. Dorothy could hardly believe what her psychic eyes were showing her.

"When I asked for a vision showing me how I was to pay my bills, I certainly didn't expect to see Marc in my vision. He didn't have any money, he had declared bankruptcy, hadn't he?

"The pictures in my mind were as clear as if I were watching a television drama. There was Marc. He was walking into a bank that I was very familiar with. I watched intently as Marc registered his name, and entered the safety deposit vault. He opened a box numbered 452. It was filled with money and United States Savings Bonds. I was so excited that I didn't sleep all night. I could hardly wait to telephone Marc the next morning.

"His reaction was just as I had expected—a complete denial that he had money hidden anywhere. I really savored the moment when I casually mentioned how he would be sent to a federal penetentiary for falsifying his bankruptcy claim if it were found that Safety Deposit Box 452 held money and bonds that belonged to him. There was dead silence on the other end of the phone.

"Needless to say, Marc withdrew his bankruptcy claim and paid back the loan of $8,000, plus $1,000 in interest.

"If it hadn't been for Visual-Telemetry I would never have gotten my money back. I was so desperate, that I hate to think of what might have happened to me if I hadn't recovered my money."

Dorothy's is an unusual story, but the happy ending is not at all unusual. You have every right to expect these same miraculous results when you *look* through Visual-Telemetry's window into the future.

VISUAL-TELEMETRY AND THE ROLE OF MEDITATION

Many forms of psychic and occult training demand that the student devote a great deal of time to meditation—the technique by which one becomes completely passive and oblivious to physical surroundings. The role of meditation in *Psychic*

Telemetry is an insignificant part of your psychic development program.

There are a few instances where you might become a passive observer as your spiritual Genie does the work, but in most cases you will want to remain as mentally alert as possible. You will be literally bombarded with Visual-Telemetry visions. You will *feel* and *hear* forces that are not physically present. Maintaining a keen alertness insures that none of the psychic information being fed to you from the Cosmic Mind goes undetected.

Many people find it very tempting to just drift away as they perform their Pillars of Power Rituals. At a previous class, a student described his feelings to his fellow classmates.

> "I feel so darned good after I perform one of my *Psychic Telemetry* Rituals, that I really have to use all of my willpower to keep myself from mentally floating away.
>
> "It sure is tempting to forget about the purpose of the Ritual—to forget about everything, as a matter-of-fact. But you have to pay attention and stay alert if you want to perform any miracles. My Guardian Genii have complained more than once that I was ignoring them."

The student is absolutely correct. Don't meditate any longer than what is called for in your various *Psychic Telemetry* Rituals.

EVERYONE HAS VISUAL-TELEMETRY POWER BUT FEW USE IT

Visual-Telemetry is not unusual. You experienced your first visions shortly after birth. You learned to subdue these visions from fear of becoming a target of wrath or ridicule from many adult members of your family, who either did not understand, or feared psychic instincts.

Most people continue to stumble through their adult lives, subduing this great Visual-Telemetry power that could set them free from any problem that might confront them.

You are fortunate because you no longer need to stumble along. The answer to every need, every wish, and every desire is yours for the asking by just using Visual-Telemetry's magical window into the future.

Don't feel that you have to prove your Visual-Telemetry powers to anyone. Skeptics constantly ask for proof, proof, and more proof! Let your miracles stand as proof of your powers. Don't waste your time on the skeptics. Your time is valuable, and better spent in performing positive, constructive miracles.

CURTIS H. WATCHED A MISSOURI TORNADO FROM HIS CALIFORNIA LIVING ROOM

Distance is not a barrier to experiencing Visual-Telemetry visions. You can close your eyes and clearly see scenes from hundreds, even thousands of miles away.

What was originally planned as a social evening among business associates quickly turned into an impromptu *Psychic Telemetry* class, as often happens at the first mention of psychic or occult powers.

On an early summer evening in California, my wife and I joined mutual friends and business associates at a party honoring an out-of-state corporation executive.

During the course of the evening, conversation drifted to the subject of my magazine writing and to the *Psychic Telemetry* classes I was then teaching in the city. It was only a matter of minutes before I was persuaded to show the group what *Psychic Telemetry* was all about. I explained how I couldn't possibly cover all of the facets of *Psychic Telemetry* in one evening, but would be happy to show them how to experience Visual-Telemetry. After a few words of instruction and explanation, I asked the group to perform the Visual-Telemetry Ritual of the Visons.

There were some people in the group who were, to say the least, less than enthusiastic as they performed the simple Ritual. One after another said, "I don't believe it. I must be imagining things. This can't be real."

Visual-Telemetry

Every person, skeptic or not, experienced at least one simple Visual-Telemetry vision. Many of the visions were of a personal nature, and not shared with the group as a whole. But the vision received by Curtis H. astounded the party goers.

Curtis began explaining his vision by prefacing his remarks with, "I think I'm crazy, but here goes!"

"This may sound strange, but when we finished the Ritual, I saw myself walking up this country road. I don't know how I knew it, but I knew that I was in Missouri.

"I had only taken a few steps before I found myself at a long driveway with a mailbox beside it. The post of the mailbox wasn't buried in the ground as you would expect. Someone had laid an old tire on the ground and filled its center with cement. The pole to the mailbox was cemented into this tire and was painted bright red. The mailbox itself was painted white.

"When I looked up the driveway, I saw a 1949 Plymouth automobile that was painted a very pale blue. Its license plates were from Oklahoma, rather than from Missouri.

"The first house was very old and built of wood. There was little paint left on the boards, but I could see that it was once painted white.

"The front of the house faced north, and I was impressed with the very steep slope to the roof, which seemed very unusual for that part of the country. The roof wasn't shingled. It was made of large sheets of aluminum.

"About a hundred feet further back from the house, I could see the remains of a smaller house, which was obviously much older than its larger companion."

A loud gasp from an attorney in our group interrupted Curtis' story. "My God!" the astonished lawyer said. "You've described my old family farm perfectly. Even the old blue Plymouth with the Oklahoma license is right. It belongs to the people whom I leased the farm to."

I asked Curtis if there was anything else in his Visual-Telemetry vision? "Well yes," he replied, "but it really sounds silly." I encouraged him to continue relating the account of his, at least so far, 100 percent accurate vision.

> "Just after I looked at the ruin of the older house, I glanced at the horizon and saw a tornado moving swiftly toward the farm.
> "I then ran to the front porch of the occupied house, yelling for the people inside to get out. Then my vision ended."

The attorney asked Curtis when he thought the tornado would occur. "I'm not sure I believe what's happening," Curtis replied. "I really think that the tornado has already hit the farm, or is just about to. But the more I think of it," Curtis continued, "the more I feel it is going to happen tonight."

The attorney was obviously shaken by Curtis' revelation. I encouraged the attorney to call the Missouri farm to give its occupants a warning.

The lawyer was filled with doubt about the accuracy of the vision, so he thought up an excuse to call the farm tenants. He was embarassed to admit to them the real reason for his call. During the course of the telephone conversation, he casually mentioned how he had heard on the news that there was a tornado watch for that area of Missouri. His face paled when the man at the other end of the line confirmed that yes, indeed, there was a tornado watch for that area.

"While I'm still on the phone, why don't you look outside and tell me what the weather's like?" the attorney anxiously asked.

The man on the farm in Missouri laid the telephone down to look at the weather outside, but he didn't come back to the telephone—at least not that night.

Everyone at the party was on edge, wondering what had happened. Why did the telephone go dead? Two days passed before there was an answer.

Visual-Telemetry

When the farmer looked out the window the night of the telephone call from California, he saw the same tornado that Curtis had seen in his vision. He quickly gathered his family around him and ran from the house. There was no storm cellar, so the quick-thinking farmer threw his family into a shallow irrigation ditch.

The tornado hit the farm. It levelled the house, the barn, and all of the sheds on the property. The old Plymouth bounced around like a rubber ball. Everything in the tornado's path was destroyed. The Missouri farmer and his family, huddled safely in the ditch, were saved from certain destruction by a Visual-Telemetry vision!

HOW A PSYCHIC TELEMETRY WORKER OPERATES

Curtis did not wear mystic robes, nor did he appear to be eccentric when he received his lifesaving vision.

A follower of *Psychic Telemetry* looks and behaves no differently than anyone else—at least on the surface. But behind those quiet eyes lies a powerhouse of occult knowledge—a mind that can see events taking place hundreds of miles away, a mind that can see the future as clearly as the present. And as these visions of the future unfold, the follower of *Psychic Telemetry* knows that he can change the future if it is not to his liking. If the futuristic panorama is pleasant, he can smugly sit back and wait for those blessings to enter his life in their certain but proper order.

DO SOME PEOPLE HAVE MORE VISUAL-TELEMETRY POWER THAN OTHERS?

There are, at times, individuals who do appear to have more *Psychic Telemetry* power than others, but this is only an *appearance*, not necessarily a reality.

It is true that you will occasionally find an extremely adept student who seems to stand out among the crowd. Investigation will reveal that he or she stands out because he or she is more vociferous—not because he or she receives more accurate Visual-Telemetry information than the silent student who quietly sits back and just smiles, *knowing* all the while.

However, you will discover that the more you use Visual-Telemetry, the more psychic information you will gather. The speed at which you receive your visions will also increase with greater use. Speed isn't necessary, but there will be times when it can be very handy.

One of my students was invited to appear on a television talk show to demonstrate Visual-Telemetry before a live audience. The hostess of the television show was very favorably inclined toward *Psychic Telemetry,* and my student accepted the invitation.

After the usual introductions, chit-chat, etc., the student was asked to demonstrate his Visual-Telemetry powers by giving predictions of the future to the audience. The moderator asked that he give his predictions quickly, so that as many people in the audience as possible might benefit from his powers.

The television hostess, the camera crew, the audience, and the station manager were awe-struck as the student stood up, and talking as quickly as his tongue would move, gave an astounding 96 predictions in just 19 minutes.

Aside from being able to talk fast, what was the student's secret for his ability to give such a large number of predictions in such a short space of time? There was no secret at all. He simply relied upon Telemetric Sign Language. The same magical language that *you* will be learning in this next exciting chapter of *<u>Psychic</u>* *<u>Telemetry</u>.*

Chapter Four

How to Read Telemetric Sign Language from the Cosmic Mind

You can now see into the future. With your Visual-Telemetry power, you are able to clearly see what is happening at a distance—just as the world famous psychics and seers are doing.

Many of the most famous seers speak of the *symbols* they receive when giving their predictions concerning the future. The symbols to which they refer are *signs* from the Cosmic Mind. They are the Telemetric Sign Language.

A symbol is *something that stands for or suggests something else by reason of its relationship or association.* For *Psychic Telemetry,* a symbol is Cosmic Sign Language. It is a picture that is worth a thousand words. It is a method used by the Cosmic Mind to transfer to you valuable and completely accurate predictions of the future.

You will be using Telemetric Sign Language long before you have completed reading this chapter. And I'm going to show you how easy it really is.

There will be no more wishing that you could give predictions equal to those published by America's famous psychics, seers, and astrologers. I guarantee that you will be able to give more accurate predictions than any of these. Newspapers and magazines pay these occultists hundreds, even thousands of dollars for the right to publish their predictions and you'll be outpredicting them every time.

HOW STEVE R. SAW AN UPCOMING VACANCY AT HIS PLACE OF WORK AND GAINED A BIG PROMOTION

Steve R. was employed by an international manufacturing organization. He worked hard, but his chances for a promotion looked pretty slim. And though his salary was adequate, there was never enough left over for vacations, new automobiles, or for many of the smaller luxuries that make life worth living.

"One evening I was sitting quietly, just relaxing," Steve related. "I really made no effort to receive any revelations or messages from the Cosmic Mind, and was surprised when symbols which I recognized as Telemetric Sign Language began to enter my consciousness.

"I saw arrows, buildings, suitcases, pencils, etc. The Cosmic Mind was using Telemetric Sign Language to show me that within a year I would be promoted at work and transferred to a manufacturing facility in another state. All of this seemed unlikely at the time. For one thing, the company I worked for didn't have a plant in the state that my symbols said I would be transferred to."

It seemed unlikely that Steve would be transferred, but he believed his Telemetric Sign Language. It had never been wrong before, and he knew it wouldn't be wrong this time. The only question in his mind was *how* these startling changes would enter his life.

"The morning after my Telemetric vision," he continued, "I was reading the newspaper at the breakfast table. There was a small article in the financial page saying there were rumors in the industry that the company for which I worked had developed a revolutionary new technology."

How to Read Telemetric Sign Language

Steve now knew how his vision would come true, and he didn't hesitate in laying the groundwork.

"The first thing I did was to talk to the company's vice-president in charge of manufacturing. I told him that I wanted a job in the new division that would be created, and that I would like to be transferred to the new plant when it was built."

The company vice-president denied that there were plans to create a new division within the company. "If the company is going to build a new plant, I certainly haven't heard about it," the company executive said.

Steve chuckled to himself. Telemetric Sign Language had shown him the future, and he felt rather smug about having so much information on the company's confidential plans.

He didn't wait for any public announcement of the company's plans. He read every book he could find on the new technology, and went to night school to enforce the knowledge that he accumulated.

"I kept the big shot informed of the progress I was making in my research. I really wasn't surprised when he called me to his office for a conference."

"Steve," the boss said, "I've been appointed to head the manufacturing operation of our new technology. The company is going to acquire property in Colorado.

"You've really impressed me with your drive and knowledge of the product. Would you be willing to transfer and take the job as my staff assistant? Your salary would be $600 a week. Think it over and let me know."

Steve didn't have to think it over. He had made up his mind the night he received his foreknowledge of the future in specifically accurate Telemetric Sign Language.

"The salary I was offered was more than satisfactory. I was making $310 a week at the time of the offer. The $600-a-week salary meant an additional $290 each week. That added up to an extra $15,000 a year. My Prosperity Genie told me that I would soon be earning another $15,000 a year, but I put it out of my mind as being totally unrealistic. I should have known better than to question my Prosperity Genie."

"If it hadn't been for Telemetric Sign Language, I would never have been promoted to a job that paid a salary of over $30,000 a year."

COSMIC MIND SPEAKS IN SYMBOLS, NOT IN WORDS

We are fortunate that the Cosmic Mind speaks in Sign Language. So much can be said with one picture. A very few pictures can tell you more than many pages of written instruction. It's very easy to see the future when it's written in Telemetric Sign Language. And it really makes a lot of sense, as you will soon discover for yourself. No long dissertations are needed to *tell* you of the future. A few simple pictures accurately *show* you the future.

TELEMETRIC SIGN LANGUAGE IS EASY

It only takes a few minutes a day to learn the complete Telemetric Sign Language. Remember, the symbols used in Telemetric Sign Language are Visual-Telemetry pictures that stand for, or suggest, something else.

Here's an example. In Telemetric Sign Language, a bee represents prosperity. If the bee in your vision is moving toward you, it means prosperity is coming. If the bee is moving away from you, it denotes loss.

A clock face in your Telemetric vision denotes months and days, not hours and minutes. The small hand of the clock points to months, the larger hand to days.

If, in seeking answers to questions regarding the future you were to see a bee moving toward you, followed by a clock whose hands showed 10:15, you have been given a revelation—"Prosperity is coming to you on October 15th." The bee means prosperity; the small hand of the clock at 10 designates October, the tenth month; the large hand of the clock at 15 denotes the fifteenth day of the month.

See how easy it is? And it's fun as well as accurate. All great prophets of the past received their revelations in allegorical symbols, and you're going to do the same thing.

HOW TO KNOW WHAT IS HAPPENING ANYWHERE IN THE WORLD

Most world events happen without really affecting you, but at times it is useful to know what is happening at other places within the universe.

At the present time, you can already see what's happening from a distance through Visual-Telemetry. You can, if you want to, use Telemetric Sign Language to forecast the results of elections, horse races, etc. Your forecasting of national events is done in the same way as foretelling your own individual future. Making world predictions is good practice, but using Telemetric Sign Language to learn your own future and to map its course is the most profitable way to use your new psychic knowledge.

HOW TO READ TELEMETRIC SIGN LANGUAGE

Your Visual-Telemetry pictures will come to you rapidly in Sign Language used by the Cosmic Mind. These visions of the future are easily understood, and appear in this following example.

This daffodil symbolizes Spring.

In Telemetric Sign Language, a bird represents good news.

A key is a new opportunity.

How to Read Telemetric Sign Language

The two buildings foretell a change of jobs.

This important arrow shows that the job in question is away from your present location.

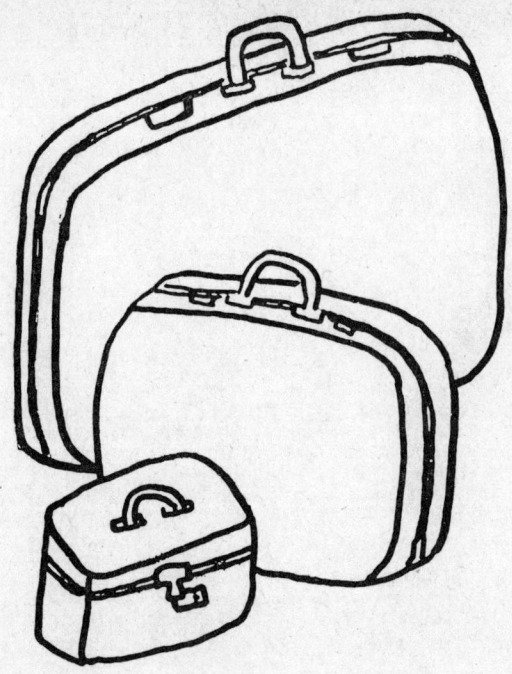

Suitcases represent travel.

In a Telemetric vision, these six Symbols would flash into your mind in seconds, but they give you an important prophesy of the future.

"In the Spring (daffodil), there will be good news (bird) about a new opportunity (key) that will be opening up.

"The opportunity will involve a change of jobs (two buildings). The new job is away from your present location (the arrow pointing away), but you will travel to that new area (suitcases)."

Once you get the hang of it, Telemetric Sign Language is one of the easiest psychic talents you will ever acquire. It's simple, but terribly important in predicting the future through Sign Language conversations with the Cosmic Mind.

TELEMETRIC SIGN LANGUAGE IS SIMPLE TO LEARN

Telemetric Sign Language is simple because *you* determine with what signs the Cosmic Mind will speak to you.

Symbols can mean different things to different people. To a deeply religious person, a bell might mean spiritual upliftment. But to the man who works during the night hours, a bell ringing early on a Sunday morning might mean loss of sleep, or annoyance.

HOW TO BEGIN YOUR TELEMETRIC LANGUAGE LESSON

Your first step is to make a list of those things that you will most often be asking about. When this list is complete, write the Symbol next to the corresponding word. Here is a fairly typical example from a student who has given me a copy of his own Telemetric Language.

SYMBOL	*INTERPRETATION*
Moving hands	Work
Still hands	Lack of work or unemployment
Two buildings	Change of jobs
Arrow pointing toward me	Someone, or something, coming to me
Arrow pointing away	Someone, or something, in another geographical area
Suitcases	Movement
Pine Tree	A strong personality
Frog	Jealousy
Books	Education
Fox	Slyness, deceit
Garbage can	Scandal
Bell	Victory, joy
Bird	Good news

Mountain	Struggle
Candle	Spiritual faith
Owl	Spiritual wisdom
Horse	Earthly wisdom
Elephant	Physical strength
Rose	Love, appreciation
Cross	Protection
Circle	Completeness
Key	A new opportunity, chance
Door	New experiences
Stairs	An easy climb
Saucer	Something left over, incomplete
Ticket	Acceptance
Signature	Binding agreement, contract
Sunflowers	Interest in Indian history
Sword	Interest in medieval history
Triangle	Interest in metaphysics
Red Cross	Involvement in medicine, healing
Blue Cross	Spiritual leader
Yellow Cross	Philosopher, philosophy

The young man who allowed me to use a portion of his Telemetric Sign Language has obviously written his language to serve his own purposes and needs. If you wish to use his Symbols, it's perfectly correct to do so. Or, you can use part or none of them.

When making your own list of Symbols, the most obvious questions to ask are those concerning such important matters as health, work, prosperity, home, and children. And for these situations, make sure you develop a useful Sign Language.

HOW TO BEGIN USING YOUR TELEMETRIC SIGN LANGUAGE

The important thing is to develop a basic group of symbols (you can add to your list as the need arises). When these symbols

How to Read Telemetric Sign Language

are established, it is only necessary to perform a simple Ritual, and the Cosmic Mind will converse with you via *Psychic Telemetry* Sign Language.

THE TELEMETRIC SIGN LANGUAGE RITUAL

Sit quietly, with back straight, and feet flat upon the floor. Your listing of symbols should be resting upon your knees. When you have become relaxed, repeat the words of this simple but powerful Ritual.

"I affirm that from this day forward, Cosmic Mind will speak clearly to me.
"I will see and understand all Symbols that are revealed to me by this great, all-knowing power."

Now read aloud your list of symbols and their interpretation. When the reading of your symbols has been completed, bring your Ritual to a close.

"I give thanks that Cosmic Mind will respond to my every need, and to my every quest, through Telemetric Sign Language. And so it is!"

Use this same Ritual any time you wish to add new symbols to your Telemetric Sign Language.

At this point, it would be useful to create a Guardian Genie whose sole duty is to help you memorize and develop a useful and complete Telemetric Sign Language. Whenever you are confronted by an unfamiliar symbol, call your Guardian Genie to you by name and ask for clarification.

RYAN R. USED TELEMETRIC SIGN LANGUAGE TO PREDICT A NEW DISCOVERY IN ASTRONOMY

Ryan R. didn't want to accept challenges when people doubted his psychic abilities, but found himself badgered into one on New Year's Eve.

Ryan performed his Visual-Telemetry Ritual, and silently prayed that the Cosmic Mind respond to his needs. "Show me a scene from the future," he said aloud. In an instant, a series of symbols flashed through his mind. He knew that his prophecy would be correct, and it was.

Ryan's prediction was that a new star would be discovered in San Jose, California. "It has something to do with the southwest, and the star I speak of is in the heavens," he firmly stated. "It will be a 'first.' "

Many people laughed at Ryan's prediction. The general feeling was that it was nearly impossible to believe that any scientific discoveries were going to be made in San Jose concerning astronomy.

A month later, there were some loud "gulps" when the San Jose newspaper reported how San Jose's Lick Observatory had performed a "first" in astronomy. It had successfuly photographed a particular type of star—a Pulsar. The article also noted that this Pulsar was generally called the "southwest composition."

An astounding prediction? Not when you rely upon Psychic Telemetry Sign Language to predict national, local, or individual future events.

HOW TO DIFFERENTIATE BETWEEN SYMBOLIC PICTURES AND ACTUAL EVENTS

Visual-Telemetry is a very versatile psychic ability. You can use it to see what's happening at a distance, and you use it to peer into the future. On the surface, it would appear difficult to tell the difference between a vision showing actual happenings, and a vision that is given in Telemetric Sign Language.

The Cosmic Mind, always working in an efficient manner, has given us a safeguard. With practice, you can move from reality to Sign Language and back again with perfect ease. The Cosmic Mind always precedes a Psychic Language message with a black dot. This black dot is a mystery, but seeing this black dot in a symbolic vision is the sure sign of an experienced seer.

How to Read Telemetric Sign Language 83

Telemetric Sign Language appears in your psychic vision to look much like a picture upon a television screen. Your first mental picture will be that of a black dot. The black dot will appear at the right side of your mental television screen, and move across your vision to the left until it disappears. This black dot will be rapidly followed by sets of Symbols. This is a symbolical message from the Cosmic Mind.

When the communication is complete, you will be shown another black dot. If this black dot is followed by additional pictures, you can be sure that you are seeing literal people, places, or things, exactly as you have previously experienced in your Visual-Telemetry Rituals.

SENSORY-TELEMETRY

In the previous chapter, you learned to use Visual-Telemetry; in this chapter, you have learned to speak the Telemetric Sign Language. But this chapter would not be complete without instruction in using the powerful techniques of two additional psychic talents, one of which is Sensory-Telemetry.

HOW JOACHIM V. THWARTED THE ATTEMPTS OF A VICIOUS CO-WORKER TO HAVE HIM DISMISSED FROM HIS WELL-PAYING JOB

Joachim V. was living in Munich, Germany, when I first heard from him. His lengthy letter was in very correct German. His letter had been translated and forwarded to me by his sister, who lived in the United States.

Joachim's sister had previously attended a *Psychic Telemetry* class. She attained so many remarkable results from the class, that she translated the class pamphlets into her native tongue and mailed them to her brother in Munich.

Joachim enjoyed working, but desired a better-paying job in the factory. He used a Telemetry Enchantment, and was quickly offered the job he desired. He excelled in his job and became the favorite of management and workers. He became so respected by his fellow employees, that he was elected to sit as the employee representative on the company's board of directors. But there was one employee who became so envious of Joachim's success, that he vowed to get him fired.

"Hans did everything he could to get me dismissed," Joachim wrote to me. "He sabotaged my work and he started vicious rumors. He even hid company tools in my lunch box, hoping it would appear that I was guilty of theft. But thanks to my Sensory-Telemetry power, he was never successful in his devious plans. I always *sensed* what his plans were, and interrupted them before they could bear fruit."

HOW TO USE SENSORY TELEMETRY

Sensory-Telemetry is the power to *feel,* or to intuitively *sense* what is about to happen. It would be the rare individual indeed who could testify that he has never had a *feeling* about a person, a place, or a thing.

Sensory-Telemetry is essentially "woman's intuition," or the "hunch" as this experience is called by the male. You do not see pictures and you do not hear sounds. Sensory-Telemetry is something that you *sense* to be true.

Everyone experiences Sensory-Telemetry at one time or another. But one time or another is not adequate when you are using *Psychic Telemetry* powers. Sensory-Telemetry can only be considered as completely constructive when it can be used at any required time. The Sensory-Telemetry Ritual ensures that your power to *sense* is always keenly active in all of your endeavors.

THE SENSORY-TELEMETRY POWER RITUAL

Perform your Pillar of Power Ritual exactly as you did in your Visual-Telemetry Ritual, and visualize your Magic Tele-Triangle. (Don't forget to perform your Second Pillar of Power Ritual, calling upon your Guardian Genie.)

Rather than concentrating on the bottom point of the traingle, you should now concentrate on its right point. This is

How to Read Telemetric Sign Language   85

the point of the triangle from which your Sensory-Telemetry power flows. When you are deep in concentration upon the right point of your Magic Tele-Triangle, repeat this powerful chant three times in quick succession.

>"I am in tune with the Infinite power of Good.
>I sense and I know all things that will bring me satisfaction.
>I am protected from all danger, both now and forevermore.
>I now command that this be so!"

It is unlikely that you will find the need to perform your Sensory-Telemetry Ritual at frequent intervals.

Most students find that their power to *sense* has become so acute, that they discover that performing the Sensory-Telemetry Ritual once every few months is adequate.

SENSORY-TELEMETRY IS YOUR CAUTION LIGHT AGAINST DANGER

You need not worry about running into the unexpected when your Sensory-Telemetry powers are at work. A caution light will flash before you. You will *sense* that something is amiss. When this warning light flashes, stop! Stop as quickly as possible, and use your other *Psychic Telemetry* powers to discover what the problem or danger is, and avoid it! "To be forewarned is to be forearmed" is a literal truth. Take advantage of it. It will never let you down.

WHEN MEDICAL SCIENCE FAILED, GORDON P. USED SENSORY-TELEMETRY TO DIAGNOSE HIS OWN ILLNESS

Gordon P. had always been a robust and healthy man. He often bragged about never being sick a day in his life. So he wasn't too disturbed when he began experiencing mild headaches.

As the weeks rolled by, Gordon's head pain became worse and worse. He finally found that he could not function properly when he was overcome by the headaches, and would take to his bed for days. A physical examination by an internist failed to show any reason for Gordon's acute pain. He next visited a neurosurgeon, who hospitalized Gordon for extensive testing. Gordon explained:

"That week I spent in the hospital was the worst week of my life," Gordon explained. "I was tested and X-rayed for hours each day. Many of the tests were not only dangerous, but extremely painful. They did tests that I had never even heard of."

At the end of a week, Gordon was released from the hospital.

"The neurologist couldn't find any reason for the terrible pain I was experiencing, so he sent me home with a large supply of pain killers.

"I was almost ready to believe that my pain was imaginary, but the doctors convinced me otherwise. They knew that my pain was real.

"Prior to the onset of a severe headache, my blood pressure and my body temperature would drop to dangerously low levels. It was finally deduced that the degree of pain that I experienced could be measured by my body temperature. The lower my temperature dropped, the more severe the pain.

Gordon was finally directed to the medical school of a large university. Extensive testing at the hospital attached to the medical school still failed to show results.

"By the time the tests were completed at the University, I was a mental and physical wreck. My headaches were destroying my entire life, and no one could even discover their origin.

"I'd better back up for a minute.

"When I first went to the doctor about my headaches, I told him that I believed the origin of my headaches could be discovered in my blood. When he asked me why I thought so, I could only reply that it was just something I *knew*, it was something that I could just *sense* was wrong. And I told every other doctor the same thing.

How to Read Telemetric Sign Language 87

"All of the physicians had me take extensive blood tests, then they tried to assure me that there was nothing in my blood that could cause my problem.

"In my desperation, I called a friend who I knew was deeply involved with *Psychic Telemetry*. I asked him to use whatever psychic power he had to find a doctor who could help me. By this time, I was seriously considering suicide."

Gordon's friend did use his *Psychic Telemetry* power, and called him to say that his Guardian Genie for Healing had shown him a doctor's name in a Visual-Telemetry vision.

"I made an appointment with the doctor chosen by my psychic friend's Healing Genie, and a miracle began to happen. I told Dr. M. that I had this overpowering feeling that the answer to my problem could be found in my blood, and that it had something to do with lack of oxygen.

"Dr. M. ordered a relatively new type of blood test. A test that would show the level of carbon-monoxide in my bloodstream. The results of the test were a shocker. The normal percentage of carbon monoxide within the blood is 2 to 3 percent. Mine was 18 percent—a near fatal level. Thank God a doctor paid attention to what I was *sensing* and did something about it.

"There is no doubt that I would now be dead of carbon monoxide poisoning if my Sensory-Telemetry had let me down. But it didn't."

Gordon P. moved from the large city in which he lived to a smog-free city in the southwest. His health returned and he finally became free of pain. At last report, Gordon and his wife were operating a very prosperous family restaurant in Arizona.

HOW AUDIO-TELEMETRY TOLD JUDY G. WHERE TO FIND HER MISSING CHILD

Judy G. panicked when she walked out of the corner market. She had parked the baby carriage, with her infant son asleep inside it, right by the door. "I was only gone long enough to buy a loaf of bread," she told the police in a hysterical voice.

It was such a bright, warm morning, that Judy decided to take her month-old son for a short walk in his baby carriage. She remembered that she needed a loaf of bread, and thinking her son completely safe, she walked into the neighborhood grocery to get the needed item.

The attempts by the police and well-meaning neighbors to calm Judy down were futile. She was a grief-stricken, hysterical woman.

Judy was lying on her bed, sobbing, when a sudden feeling of calm overtook her.

"I don't know what happened," she related, "but one moment I was hysterical, and the next moment I felt perfectly calm and in complete control of the situation.

"I closed the bedroom door so that I could have privacy, and I performed the Audio-Telemetry Ritual. When I finished the Ritual, I waited to hear something. I was discouraged at that moment because I didn't hear a word. I thought the Ritual was a complete failure."

Judy later told friends that she was very disturbed at the failure of the Ritual.

"I was ready to fall on the bed and cry again, when I heard a voice in the hall say, *The baby's in the 600 block of South Erie.*

"I rushed from the bedroom to see who had found my son. No one was in the hallway, and the neighbor's swore that no one had even mentioned South Erie."

Judy knew that she had heard a voice, and she listened to it.

"My friends thought that I was crazy, but they followed me as I jumped in the car and sped to Erie, which was only three blocks away."

Judy found her baby safe and unharmed. Apparently, two small girls had walked by the corner grocery just as Judy parked the carriage. The girls wanted to play house, and pushed the baby and the buggy away, thinking he would be a welcome addition to their game.

Judy found her son being pampered by the two girls on the front lawn of their home. "But what would have happened when the girls tired of playing house?," Judy thought.

The whole story could have ended tragically, but thanks to Judy's knowledge of *Psychic Telemetry,* the story had a happy ending.

HOW TO USE AUDIO-TELEMETRY

Judy, in the above case history, heard a "voice" speaking in the hallway of her home. She understood Audio-Telemetry, and she made it work.

Audio-Telemetry is the hearing of sounds not present to the physical senses. These sounds can be a voice, or they can be music. This psychic rhythm can be the sound of anything, but it will not be heard by the physical ear. It is heard by the *psychic ear.*

Except on rare occasions, these sounds are heard only by the person performing the Audio-Telemetry Ritual. What you hear depends on what you ask during your Ritual. In Judy's case, she needed to hear a voice. She had a specific need and it was fulfilled.

You can use Audio-Telemetry in a hundred different ways. The "voice" will answer your every question. Do you need peaceful music to relax by? Ask for it!

As I sat writing these words, I telephoned six different people and asked them for what purposes they used Audio-Telemetry. I believe their replies are typical of the wonders you can achieve with this particular *Psychic Telemetry* phenomena.

Bob: I have a hard time falling asleep at night, so I ask for beautiful music—it's heavenly!

Betty: I sell real estate. My "voice" tells me what to offer when I'm buying.

Dan: It gets lonely driving a truck. I carry on conversations with my "voice" during the long stretches of road.

Len: I'm a doctor, and I usually rely on my own knowledge to treat my patients. But if I have a very difficult case to diagnose, I ask my "voice" for help.

Cary: Whenever I get stuck on a song lyric that I'm writing, I use Audio-Telemetry to help me out.

Claude: I use my Audio-Telemetry to win at the horse races.

THE AUDIO-TELEMETRY RITUAL

Follow the same Ritual as you did in Visual and Sensory-Telemetry. Visualize your First Pillar of Power enclosed in a large triangle.

When the Pillar is alive and pulsating, concentrate on the *left* point of the Magic Triangle. This is the point of the triangle that controls your *psychic hearing*.

When you become relaxed and have the left point of the triangle firmly within your mind, repeat these words three times:

>"**My psychic ear is open,
And now I can hear,
All of the good sounds,
That there are for me.**"

Just sit and listen! You will be wonderfully surprised at the beautiful voices, the music, and the sounds that will flood your mind and lighten your burdens.

Perform your Second Pillar of Power Ritual, and bring your ceremony to a close.

USE YOUR NEW POWERS TO MAKE EVERY DREAM COME TRUE

There you have them! Three psychic powers that will give a tremendous boost to your *Psychic Telemetry* as you practice them daily.

All of this power is yours to command, and Chapter Five gives you further advice on how to get even closer to the awesome power that you control.

Chapter Five

How to Command and Control Others with the Magic Tele-Aurascope

Most of the problems we face in life are caused by individuals. This chapter will show you how to use your Magic Tele-Aurascope to change people's moods, and even their thoughts. No longer will you have to wonder what a person is thinking or feeling. You'll know all about them in a matter of seconds.

You are about to discover one of the most fascinating and beneficial aspects of *Psychic Telemetry*—analyzing a person's character immediately, and having the power to change it at will.

JEFFREY B. SOARED FROM UNDERPAID TEACHER TO TOP EDUCATIONAL ADMINISTRATOR

Jeff was a frustrated and underpaid sixth-grade teacher who desperately hoped for advancement into educational administration. Jeff's classroom was filled with problem children, which didn't help his deep-seated frustration.

"I'm going to give up teaching at the end of this school year," he confided to me. "I work hard every day, I give the best I have to my students, but it just doesn't seem to be enough."

Performing hard work that goes unrecognized by others seems to be a common problem. But Jeff did something about his problem. He used the Magic Tele-Aurascope. In just a few months, Jeff was named "Teacher of the Year." A year later, he was promoted to a top administrative post at a salary of $40,000 a year.

Soon after his promotion, he called me on the telephone. "Thank heaven for the Magic Tele-Aurascope," he said.

THE RITUAL THAT WILL DIRECT THE MAGIC TELE-AURASCOPE

Directing the Magic Tele-Aurascope is a simple but powerful way to accomplish just about anything you want.

Place the index finger of your right hand at the middle of the forehead, and press down. At the same time that you are pressing down, begin to hum quietly with your lips closed. Continue humming until you can clearly hear the "hmmm" within your head, and feel the strong vibrations within your throat.

LOUISE L. BECAME THE BEST-LIKED GIRL IN THE OFFICE AND MARRIED THE BOSS

Louise L. answered a newspaper advertisement for an office manager, and landed the job. What Louise didn't realize, was that the other women in the office expected that one of them would be promoted to the position.

Louise's first day on the job was a disaster. The secretaries who worked for her were cold and silent. No one offered her help or encouragement. Louise was ready to resign her new job on the first day. Just at quitting time, she decided to stay on the job for one more day, and use her Magic Tele-Aurascope.

Louise drove by to see me after she left work that night. I had never seen a more depressed or dejected girl.

"As bad as I need that job, I could never work under those conditions," she said. "It wasn't only the girls—the boss looked through me like I didn't even exist." She told me of her plan to turn the full force of her Tele-Aurascope on the entire office.

"If that doesn't work, I give up!"

I had no doubts that it would work—and it did. I didn't hear from Louise for two days. She finally telephoned late one evening.

"I'm sorry that I'm calling so late, but I just got home from having dinner with my boss. I had dinner with him last night, too, but it was too late to call you after I got home from the theater. You'll never guess what happened!"

Louise had so much to tell me, and was talking so rapidly, that I had to slow her down. She told me what had happened on her second day at the job.

"I knew who the real ringleader was, and I knew that if I could break her hate and vindictiveness, that I would win the battle.

"I went to work early and focused my Magic Tele-Aurascope on Helen's desk. I filled the whole area around her desk with a vibration of friendship and helpfulness. I did the same thing to the work area of every other girl in the office.

"The next thing I did was to summon the Guardian Genie (Harry), that I use to help me influence others. Once I relied upon Harry, and my Magic Tele-Aurascope, there was no doubt that I would soon be victorious in overcoming the envy that was being directed toward me.

"Helen was the first one in to work that morning. She didn't bother to answer my 'good morning' as she hung up her coat in silence. She had a terrible scowl across her face.

"I watched as Helen sat down at her desk. A look of surprise and pleasantness soon replaced her scowl. She became very nervous and fumbled with the pencils on her desk. Very quickly she pushed back her chair and came walking up to where I was sitting. 'Louise, I feel like someone's pushing me up here. I just want to apologize for the way I've acted. You can count on me for any help you need.'

"I had to giggle to myself as each girl in the office came in to work, sat down, and, as if propelled by a great unseen force, bolted from her chair to come to me and offer her friendship.

"The Tele-Aurascope really worked. It worked so well that I decided to use it on my boss. Late in the afternoon, he walked from his office to speak to me. 'Louise, it's against office policy for the manager to date the office employees, but I was wondering if you would have dinner with me this evening, and then go to the theater?' That's why I couldn't call you until late this evening," Louise said to me over the telephone.

I recently heard that Louise married her boss and is living in a luxury apartment on San Francisco's famous Nob Hill.

HOW TO WORK WITH THE MAGIC TELE-AURASCOPE

There is an electromagnetic force which surrounds every thing within the universe. This electromagnetic force, which I term the aura, is the power that I will teach you to use and manipulate to fulfill your heart's desire.

The simple use of Visual-Telemetry, which you learned in Chapter Three, will enable you to perform instant miracles with your Magic Tele-Aurascope.

HOW HARLAN V. COMMANDED AN INSTANT APOLOGY

Harlan V. worked for a large Texas company when I first knew him. There was a constant turnover of personnel in his department because of the domineering and brutal executive who guided it.

After a particularly embarrassing and unjustified reprimand before his fellow employees, Harlan decided to do something about it. He performed his Magic Tele-Aurascope Ritual and called his Guardian Genie to his side. Silently he commanded that Mr. Big come out of his office and publicly apologize for his ill treatment of Harlan.

How to Command and Control Others

It was only seconds before the door to the Executive Suite opened. In the doorway stood an obviously flustered and embarrassed executive. "Harlan, I'd like to apologize to you in front of everyone for the things I said. I was wrong and I'm sorry."

Mr. Big didn't even know why he was apologizing—but Harlan did. No one can withstand the magic power of the Tele-Aurascope. In addition to the apology, Harlan received a 10 percent pay raise.

FAMOUS MOVIE STAR BUILDS WALL OF PROTECTION

My wife and I were having dinner at a Los Angeles hotel with one of America's most brilliant movie and television stars. The number of fans seeking autographs or the opportunity to touch Mr. X. made it impossible to eat, let alone carry on a conversation about *Psychic Telemetry,* which was the reason for the dinner.

During a break in the steady stream of fans, I suggested that we all try using our Tele-Aurascope to keep the fans at a distance, so that we might finish our dinner and have an uninterrupted conversation. I gave Mr. X. a very quick lesson in the use of the Tele-Aurascope Ritual. After a few moments of concentration, we resumed our dinner. Mr. X. said, "I can't believe it," as we watched the fans start for the table but suddenly stop before they reached us. A sheepish look would cross their faces. They almost ran back to their own tables.

Mr. X. has been a follower of *Psychic Telemetry* since that night. Though already extremely successful, Mr. X's career has soared to new heights. But more important to Mr. X., *Psychic Telemetry* gave him what his wealth had not been able to buy—peace of mind, and the ability to appear in public without being immediately mobbed by admirers.

THE MAGIC TELE-AURASCOPE'S LAW OF ATTRACTION

The old saying that "like attracts like" is true. There is a magnetic quality within the human aura that attracts to the individual the very things that they have built up within the aura. Because of this magnetism, it is extremely important that you think positively about all of the things you would like to attract into your life. This positive thinking builds power into your aura and magnetically attracts those things which you desire—whether good, or bad.

The aura is a constantly changing electromagnetic force around you. The aura reflects what you are at the precise moment. Every thought and deed performed by you will change your aura to conformity. You will learn to see and analyze the human aura in the remaining pages of this chapter. No one will ever again be able to hide his true character or motives from you.

ZOLA H. ZOOMS FROM WELFARE MOTHER TO SUCCESSFUL BUSINESS WOMAN

Zola H. was trying to raise her three children the best she could on the small amount of welfare aid that she received. Barely eking out a living was not what Zola wanted, and it wasn't what Zola wanted for her children. It appeared that Zola would be trapped in her cycle of poverty and never have more than the small amount of material possessions that she had in her dingy apartment. Zola desperately wanted better food, clothing, and cultural advantages for herself, but mostly for her children.

Zola's desire was to open a small gift and crafts shop in one of the larger shopping centers. She applied for many loans, but all were rejected because she didn't possess adequate collateral.

Zola heard about the power of the Tele-Aurascope from a friend, and decided to give it a try. She walked into the bank and focused her concentration on the loan officer. Zola concentrated with all of her might that the bank official would grant her the loan she needed to start her business. Zola could tell that the mood of the bank officer changed as she concentrated, but she became timid when the loan official seemed to return her gaze. Zola left the bank without asking for her loan.

How to Command and Control Others

As Zola returned home and was opening her door, she hurried to answer the ringing telephone. It was the loan officer from the bank calling. Zola's Tele-Aurascope was successful. The bank was calling to say that they had reconsidered Zola's request for a small business loan—even though she was considered a high risk.

Within weeks, Zola had become highly successful. She was making over $500 a week profit from her enterprise, and that isn't the end of Zola's story.

As in many businesses, Zola found that shoplifting was cutting into her profits. She spent a few minutes each day learning how to see and analyze an aura. Within days, shoplifting in her store had almost dropped to zero. She could look into the aura of the people entering her store, and instantly tell which people were inclined toward thievery. She could watch them closely—and she did. The would-be thieves nearly bolted from the store as soon as Zola gazed into their aura.

HOW TO SEE THE AURA

The human aura can be seen with the physical eyes (it appears as a reflection of light around the head). Using the Visual Telemetry learned in Chapter Three, you will see and identify the various colors that exist within the human aura, and analyze them for their various personality characteristics.

It's very simple to see the aura around any individual—you will know their true character regardless of how they act outwardly. Can they be trusted? Are they sincere? Are they prosperous? All of these things, and more will be secretly revealed to you. No longer can anyone conceal the truth from you about any thing, or any situation.

Perform Your Visual Telemetry Ritual, as taught to you in Chapter Three. After you have performed this ritual, gaze approximately six inches above the head of the individual whose aura you want to see. Do not stare, but gaze gently. Suddenly you will notice masses of pulsating color around the head. These colors will appear much as a rainbow in perpetual motion.

HELEN M. WISHED TO BE A POLICEWOMAN. HER DREAM CAME TRUE

Helen M.'s greatest desire was to be a policewoman. She was hired by a sheriff's department and put on a six-month probationary period. Helen was very unsure of her status as the months rolled by—until she learned to use the Magic Tele-Aurascope.

Helen was assigned the responsibility of transporting female prisoners to the State corrections center. Her male peers laughed, as this was known to be one of the department's toughest assignments. They thought Helen was out of her mind to drive from the jail with her female prisoner beside her in the front seat—without handcuffs. Helen did this time after time, with an occasional prisoner in the backseat behind the heavy screen. Helen passed her probationary period with flying colors. What was her secret? No secret at all.

Helen did a very simple thing upon entering the prisoner's cell to begin transport to the State prison. She looked into the prisoner's aura to see if the prisoner was trustworthy or dangerous. Helen never made one mistake.

Helen has been promoted several times since those early days. Her salary is more than she ever hoped to make, and she has a very self-satisfying job. Incidentally, Helen recently married the judge in whose court she had been assigned to temporary bailiff duty.

ALEXIS CATCHES A "CON" MAN

Alexis was a widow who had plenty of money, but was looking for wise investments to increase her nest egg. Through friends, Alexis was introduced to a religious leader who was making fabulous amounts of money for his "followers" through investments in South American silver.

Alexis looked into the "holy man's" aura, and saw characteristics opposite from those portrayed outwardly. She saw

How to Command and Control Others 99

greed, avarice, hate, etc. Alexis listened intently to the financial proposition and acted interested in this "chance-of-a-lifetime," or so the religious leader said. Alexis said that she would return the next evening with $5,000 cash.

Full of suspicion, Alexis called the attorney general of the state where the religious organization had its headquarters. There was a warrant outstanding for the man's arrest. Due to Alexis' psychic vision, the man was extradited, tried, and convicted.

Besides saving herself thousands of dollars, she was the financial savior to those who were investing their lifesavings with a holy man who would have soon disappeared had it not been for Alexis' vigilance.

And Alexis knew the true character of the phoney minister from just a 30-second glimpse at his human aura.

HOW TO ANALYZE THE HUMAN AURA

After locating the rainbow of colors around the head, mentally note those colors nearest the head. These will be the person's strongest personality characteristics. The further the color from the head, the less influence it plays in the individual's personality.

All colors specify certain personality traits. All shades of red denote physical characteristics. All blue shades denote spiritual characteristics, and yellow shades the mental. It is important to note that all *clear* colors are "positive" traits, and all colors that appear muddy or mixed with black are "negative" characteristics. Below is a Table of Colors and their meanings for your quick reference.

TABLE OF COLORS

RED (Physical)
    Bright Red   Physical strength, health, vigor.
                                This shade of red shows physical

endurance, the ability to live with small amounts of sleep. This also shows the ability to recover quickly from illnesses. There is an immunity from what are usually considered to be "contagious" diseases.

This person has a high sex drive, but might bury himself in work rather than love affairs.

Bright Red Mixed With Black

Anger (I was so angry I could see red!).

This color shows the inclination to seek revenge. This person has almost superhuman strength if his anger is directed toward destruction. This person does not follow through with promises, and is "two-faced."

The person maintaining this color has little interest in intellectual endeavors: probably drinks sporadically, but heavily.

This color shows no sense of loyalty toward friends, but an overly possessive feeling toward family.

This person is known for sarcasm, and the joy they feel when they hurt others through a biting wit.

There is a great stubborness and sense of frustration when confronted by change.

Pure Crimson

The color of pure crimson denotes a great understanding. It is the color of physical love. It is the color of one who likes physical closeness—who enjoys a handshake or a hug. This is the aura color that shows the individual is in love with one person—intensely loyal and faithful.

This person is a good parent and very affectionate toward children.

Dark Crimson

This tone of red is the negative opposite of "pure crimson."

This color is seen in the auras of those who love the sex act, but not the person. They have a subconscious desire to be unhappy in their personal relationships.

If things are going too smoothly, this individual will cause unpleasant things to occur. This person states that he cannot stand an argument, but he will be the first to provoke one.

This color shows a preferance toward darkness, the night.

Women who carry this color strongly within their aura are inclined to often change the color of their hair. Men appear to prefer wearing plaids or rectangular patterns in their clothing.

Rose

Rose is the color of an individual dedicated to the well-being of others. It is the dominant color in the auras of social workers, nurses, ministers, etc.

The person who has rose as the dominant color in his aura loves life. He has a well-developed sense of humor.

This person is compassionate and can keep a secret. These happy individuals are often unmarried and view the whole of mankind as their family.

Pink

"I'm in the 'pink' of condition" aptly describes the character and personality of the person who has pink as the dominant color within his aura.

This person is very well-balanced, is harmonious, slow to anger, generous, and kind.

This individual has a quiet nature—not because of shyness, but because he finds other people so interesting, and likes to listen rather than talk.

He will avoid conflict, will join group activity, but never lose his sense of independence.

The person who shows a dominant color of pink within the aura makes a good friend, and is talented in creative endeavors such as knitting, sewing, cooking, landscaping, carpentry, painting, and photography.

Red Orange

Red orange shows salesmanship, leadership, egotism.

This person is a real 'hustler' who must be doing several things at one time.

Red orange shows you an individual who likes pressure and works well under it.

This man or woman will "blow up" quickly, but will get over it just as quickly. They tend to be loud and pushy, but admire people who stand up to them and speak their minds.

The red-orange individual is very intolerant toward the mistakes others might make, but always has an excuse to cover his own mistakes.

Red-orange is a color commonly found in the aura of the politician.

Red-Violet
The person who has red-violet as the predominate color within their aura is inclined toward membership in lodges and societies.

This person does not work well alone, but is a ball-of-fire when participating in group activities.

Red-violet auras show an individual who likes games and enjoys the challenge found in trying to beat the odds at gambling.

Ceremonial activities hold a definite fascination for the red-violet man or woman.

POSITIVE RED TONES

Individuals who have shades of red as the dominating colors within their aura can be complex and mystifying.

The positive shades of red denote individuals who are energetic, kind, generous, and born to leadership. They are faithful friends, good lovers, and are usually prosperous. If they are not properous, it is usually by choice—they are overly generous to charities and causes that they feel to be worthwhile. These people make good executives, but can be highly critical of their employees.

The positive red tones show you the athlete, and the individual who is very conscious about the appearance of his body, is a snappy dresser, and dreads getting old. Red makes a good companion if you have the endurance to keep up with him. One day he will be quietly engrossed in a novel, the next day he might be climbing a mountain.

Positive reds will usually prefer dark, conservative colors in their dress and home furnishings, but seem to be "turned on" by the color of powder-blue. Yellow, as it is found in nature, is acceptable to these individuals, but is generally avoided in dress or furnishings. They like leather.

In stature, the "red" will stand straight, but is inclined to sit toward the front of a chair—unless it's a rocking chair! They are broad at the shoulders, but have small waists and narrow hips. When walking, their gait is fast and their toes point straight ahead.

THE NEGATIVE RED TONES

Negative Reds are a sorrowful lot and should be avoided if possible. They are usually overweight, slouch, and walk flat-footed.

These negative reds are dangerous as friends, lovers, or business associates—they will hold your feelings in low esteem. They can be heavy drinkers, rapists, and child molesters. They are unfaithful in love affairs, and not trustworthy with money.

Negative reds can turn on the charm when they need something, but will give the cold-shoulder when they have achieved their goals.

These individuals believe themselves to be the most important persons in the world. They ignore their children and their own parents. These individuals prefer the company of their own sex and boast constantly.

The negative red has little ambition or drive. He is bitter because people do not recognize what he believes to be his obvious talents. He is a slow thinker who changes his mind constantly. This person is late to appointments and undependable in business.

SPIRITUAL QUALITIES
WITHIN THE AURA

BLUE

Sky Blue — This tone of blue shows that its auric wearer maintains a positive spiritual attitude toward all of life. This blue also shows that the person is on a concise path of constant spiritual progression and evolution.

This person is never satisfied with his own spiritual growth, and is constantly in search of Higher Truths.

Sky blue men and women often neglect worldly responsibilities in their quest for spiritual knowledge.

You will find this person to be quiet and retiring. Their knowledge of spiritual Truth does not give them an evangelical nature. They believe that each man must, on his own, find the Truth that is satisfying to him.

Violet   Violet is one of the most beautiful of auric colors. It shows you an individual who has grasped spiritual knowledge, and knows how to apply this knowledge in a practical manner to improve all facets of his life.

The person who can maintain this color within the aura is a person who can face any crisis or difficult situation with grace, dignity, and head held high.

Very Dark Blue   This person is filled with superstition, and is a religious fanatic.

Dark blue people have a strong belief in hell, and an even stronger belief that any person thinking differently than they, in a religious manner, is a worker for the devil.

You will find, unfortunately, that these individuals welcome pain, poverty, and despair as opportunities to prove their faith.

Little social life is enjoyed by these fanatics. Large families and poverty are their mark in life.

Blue Gray	"I feel 'blue' today!" And usually they do. This tone of blue shows mental depression and listlessness.

This person could soon become physically ill, and would be slow to recover.

No happiness or progress can be enjoyed by the blue-gray individual until he breaks the stranglehold of self-pity and doubt that surrounds him. |
| Purple | This person loves ceremony as an observer, not as a participant.

The purple aura shows that things must be done in a proper order and a proper sequence. This person completes all tasks in a thorough and efficient manner. Tasks are sometimes completed slowly because of the attention paid to insignificant details.

The purple loves all tones of blue in physical surroundings and dress. They are occasionally attracted to the color of bright red, but this attraction is temporary and soon leaves them.

This individual is studious, but a slow reader.

Fastidiousness, neatness, and cleanliness are essential to the peace of mind and comfort of those possessing purple as the dominant color within their auras. They will flee people and places that do not show these qualities.

Chaos and untidiness are so dreadful to this person, that he will |

leave those he loves best before he will accept these negative qualities.

This person would rather hurt himself than others, but is unable to completely control his emotions.

Clear Blue   This beautiful tone of blue shows you a highly principled and moral individual. This lucky person can ward off temptation with little effort.

Scrupulous honesty surrounds this principled party. They will go to great effort to return a penny mistakenly given them.

They are very hard on themselves, graciously accepting the faults of others, but finding it difficult to forgive their own weaknesses—which are very few.

CHARACTERISTICS OF THOSE POSSESSING POSITIVE BLUE TONES

Those blessed people who possess the positive blue tones are assets to all of us. Many scientists, doctors, accountants, mathematicians, farmers, and auto mechanics possess this beautiful auric color. But the occupation of the person does little to determine these strong spiritual characteristics.

You will find that these people are difficult to live with unless you have acquired these same personality characteristics. They demand the highest from their family members and close personal associates.

These people are almost impossible to anger, but when Principle is involved, they will fight the world with what they consider to be "righteous wrath." And they are fearless.

Quietness of nature is their trademark, but they can become human dynamos when involved in a Just Cause. The positive blue person believes that hard work is good for the soul. They cannot understand or accept laziness.

Individuals possessing these tones respect all forms of life, and love the variety of blooms on flowers.

Individuals of these positive blue tones appreciate formality, like to dress well, and are sometimes offended by what they consider to be an improper use of nicknames.

The elderly receive much attention and respect from this spiritual group of people. Wealth, status, and position make little impression upon these stout-of-heart.

GENERAL CHARACTERISTICS OF NEGATIVE BLUE TONES

The negative blue tones within the aura present to you one of the most difficult people in the world to live with—they are very hypocritical in nature.

These dogmatic religionists view every unpleasant circumstance as the work of the devil, and they find great joy in their suffering, viewing it as an opportunity to show their faith.

The individuals possessing these negative tones as the primary color within their aura tend to mingle with their own. They are highly superstitious and live in constant fear of death, hell, and the devil.

These people can not be trusted if you are not a part of their group. They will lie, cheat, and steal to achieve their goals, rationalizing that it is "just" to use any means to wrest material possessions from the devil, who is you, in their eyes.

This type of person is emotionally attached to his particular Cause, and releases these emotions in sexual acts. They have a highly oversexed personality.

The negative blues usually have a large family where little love, but a great deal of discipline, is shown. They are undereducated, and have no interest in cultural pursuits.

These people tend to favor dark clothing and heavy-appearing shoes. Their hair is usually brown to very dark brown. The eyes appear smaller than average, and an unusually large number of this group wear glasses by the time they reach their early thirties.

No friends will you find here.

YELLOW (Mental)

Light Yellow

This beautiful shade of yellow is found within the aura of those individuals who have gained a high degree of intelligence. This intelligence may have been gained through formal education, or it may be self-taught.

This light yellow shows you an individual who has great appreciation toward cultural pursuits, but does not necessarily show a great interest in any particular cultural field.

This color is often seen within the aura of the teacher and of those who love music. Most of these people enjoy dancing, or the rhythmic movement in ballet and the various ethnic or tribal dances.

Light yellow is also the color of instinct and psychic power. This color pulsates dramatically through the auras of the followers of *Psychic Telemetry*. It is pulsating through your aura at this very moment. It is the basic color that dominates your aura as you learn to use your Magic Tele-Aurascope later in this chapter.

Bright Yellow

This is a mind that never stops working—it's always thinking and planning. In fact, these people sometimes talk so rapidly that it is difficult to understand them.

These bright yellow personalities make wonderful companions—if you can keep up with them. It is torture for these people to sit and relax. They feel that relaxation is a waste of time when there are so many things that they want to do.

To these individuals, money is to spend and not to invest or save. Though they have boundless energy, they will use little of this energy in business or other money-making endeavors.

Deep Yellow

Plans abound within the minds of those possessing deep yellow as the primary color within their aura. Never satisfied with the present, they are always planning for the future.

These people do not like spur-of-the-moment activities. They like their activities to be planned—to have plenty of notice before beginning any new undertaking.

These people are sociable, but generally quiet. They are not loud or boisterous. They have complete control over themselves, but can become rattled if outside influences try to force quick decisions and quick compliance. They do not like to be rushed.

These people are courteous and prompt in their appointments.

Deep yellow is commonly found within the auras of those persons having strong interests in logic, ethics, statistics, accounting and mathematics.

Gold

Gold shows you a love of pure knowledge. It is the color of the religious teacher and religious philosopher. It is the color of the individual who seeks truth in all things.

Gold does not show you a *religious* person, it shows you a *spiritual* person. There are many people who are very religious, but lack true spirituality.

These individuals enjoy being alone to meditate and pray. They are tolerant and loving. They have a strong and uncompromising character.

These people do not appear timid and meek, for they are not. They have confidence in themselves and life.

Do not try to push these golden auras. They are fearless and have the courage of a lion.

Many of these people marry and make good mates, *if* you do not expect or demand a romantic love.

They are intensely loyal, and they love animals.

A large majority of these individuals are blue-eyed and of fair complexion.

Yellow-Orange   This person is very persuasive, but will rarely argue. Known for his willingness to compromise, he rarely demands that things be done his way.

This person has a healthy ego, but is not inclined to dominate—and he will not accept domination from others.

Here you can find a good friend. A friend who is a good listener and will rarely give advice, unless he is asked.

The yellow-orange shows pride, but not arrogance. If there is a job to do, he will finish it. But he is not ruled by detail.

POSITIVE QUALITIES OF THOSE HAVING YELLOW AS THEIR DOMINANT COLOR

If you want the intelligent, the suave, and the sophisticated around you, you want to draw those people to you possessing the positive yellow tones within their aura.

These positive yellow individuals are the civilizers of society in an intellectual manner (they are not, however, the civilizers in the strong family sense).

Here we have the community organizers, though they are somewhat selfish in their goals and the causes to which they apply their energy.

These are generally good mates, but are not the best of lovers. They have many acquaintances, but very few good friends. These intellectuals have a tendency to expect much from their immediate families, but are overly tolerant toward the faults of those outside of their family domain.

The men who carry this positive yellow as the dominant color within the aura are overly indulgent toward their daughters, but have poor relationships with their sons. There appears to be little closeness between these fathers and their sons.

Women are the exact opposite. They have full and meaningful relationships with their sons, but find it difficult to understand their daughters, which in turn leads to a great deal of personal animosity.

THE NEGATIVE YELLOW TONES

Immaturity, constantly changing personalities, nervousness, and mental illness are the strong personality characteristics of those carrying these negative yellow tones within their auras.

It is very difficult to feel at ease with these negative individuals. Their emotional state is never static—it changes from minute to minute. These individuals can have a very cruel nature.

Lasting relationships are rare, even within the family. They are constant drifters who seldom communicate with either friend or family. These are often the people who need help, and they know it, but they rarely accept the help that they need.

These negative yellows are interested in sex as a mental endeavor, and feel very little emotional satisfaction from this type of romance. They enjoy discussing and comparing their sexual encounters with anyone who will listen. They can not keep a secret where a sexual matter is concerned. If you value your reputation, you should keep these negative yellow tones at a good distance.

None of your beliefs are safe from attack. This person will go to the greatest lengths to persuade you to change your belief about the most unimportant of details.

THE GLORIOUS GREEN

The color green is a combination of blue and yellow. But its importance in the proper analysis of the auric colors makes it more reasonable to set it apart from, rather than combine with yellow or blue.

Much can be learned from the green tones—especially concerning health, emotions, home, and children.

GREEN

Mixed Green	"I feel green around the gills!" is an apt expression for describing this dark, mixed green within the aura.
	This tone denotes poor health—a person who is not up to par, either physically or mentally.
	Due to their poor health, these persons can become cross and demanding.

This person is a "real drag" to be around, and he can quickly deplete you of your own energy.

Light Green Light green shows you great tolerance. Though this tolerance is toward all things, it is primarily directed toward children and the elderly. This person is filled with emotional love, and makes an ideal marriage partner.

Light green is also the vivid color of those who make excellent parents.

How these people love a home! They do not love a house for its grandeur, but by the feeling they create within. These fortunate people can make a loving home in one room or in a mansion.

Clear Green Clear green is the color of healing. It is manifested in the auras of those who are being healed, but usually it is in the auras of those who have the ability to heal. This person can perform healings such as those described in Chapter Seven of this book.

Forest Green Love of nature. Love of animals. The environmentalist, farmer, forester, etc., are those whom you will meet when seeing this glossy forest green within the aura.

Though these people are a bit disorganized, they make wonderful friends. But think twice before you chose one as a business partner—unless it is a venture concerning the out-of-doors.

Dull Green	Here we have malice, insincerity, and the liar. They are untrustworthy and make neither friend, lover or marriage partner. They dislike children and the elderly. They scheme and plan ways in which they might take advantage of others. No good relationships can evolve from association with these dull green individuals.

MISCELLANEOUS AURA COLORS

BROWN

Clear Brown	This color shows you that you are with a materially prosperous and industrious individual.
Dull Brown	With dull, mixed brown, we find a selfish and miserly person. He thinks more of money than any person in the world. This person is spiritually corrupt.
Grey	Extremely negative thoughts. A very unreliable person.
White	Pure spirit (God). This person has achieved the highest of spiritual attainment. It is rare that you will ever see this color within the aura.
Black	Hatred, revenge, and pessimism are the dominant characteristics of this personality.

KNOW ALL THERE IS TO KNOW ABOUT EVERY PERSON YOU MEET

You can now see and recognize everything there is to know about every person. No one can deceive you again. You'll never be disillusioned by anyone again. You will know exactly who they are at every minute.

HOW TO USE YOUR MAGIC TELE-AURASCOPE TO MAKE OTHERS DO YOUR BIDDING

Now that you know what each color in the aura means, you can easily change the thoughts and personalities of others to what you want them to be. You might call this your aura "zap" gun.

To change another person's personality or to make him do your bidding, it's only necessary for you to follow these simple steps:

1. Close your eyes and visualize the light yellow color of your own psychic power.
2. Mentally move this color of power into the aura of the person you choose to influence, even if the person is at a distance.
3. Once you have firmly placed this powerful force within their aura, mentally demand that it explode into the color you desire. For example, if you want tolerance, make your demand light green. If you are seeking physical love, demand that the appropriate shade of red explode within the aura. Ask your Guardian Genie to add his power to this psychic explosion.
4. Just sit back and enjoy your miraculous success. Within seconds, minutes at the most, you will have a willing, obedient slave.

Chapter Six

Tele-Psychometry–Divining Miracle Power from Inanimate Objects

Inanimate objects are not just dead *things!* Inanimate objects are full of *life!* They vibrate, tingle, and sparkle. They all have a story to tell, and they're waiting to tell their unique and fascinating stories to you.

Would you like to walk into a house and have it tell you its story? Would you like to pick up a vase in a second-hand store and listen to its tale of having traveled the seven seas? You'll do this and a hundred more things before you have finished this powerful chapter on the miracles of Tele-Psychometry.

HOW INANIMATE OBJECTS TALK TO YOU

Inanimate objects do not have a voice to talk to you, nor do they have a brain with which to think. But inanimate objects do have an etheric memory. You will learn to tap this etheric memory by using the Visual-Telemetry, Audio-Telemetry, and Sensory-Telemetry powers learned in earlier chapters of this book.

Tele-Psychometry is the divination of known past or present facts which surround an object or objects. Everything within the universe has a character or nature of its own. The character (etheric memory) of inanimate objects is determined not only by the physical environment around them, but more strongly by the thoughts, words, and emotions expressed around these objects by people. It is these thoughts, feelings, etc. expressed around the object, that cling to it to create the etheric memory with which you will converse through various *Psychic Telemetry* techniques. Essentially, you will be reading the soul or character of an object.

This chapter on Tele-Psychometry will be one of the most pleasurable adventures of your life.

HAROLD C. HELPS POLICE SOLVE BIZARRE MURDERS

This true case history received so much publicity, and the people involved were so famous, that I have changed the names and the location of this ghastly event so unpleasant memories need not be stirred within the minds of those family and friends who remain.

I do not enjoy writing of this horrible tale, but it is positive proof of inanimate objects retaining memories. It is startling proof of what the power of Tele-Psychometry can do, even under the most trying of circumstances.

On a Tuesday afternoon, the police heard a hysterical female voice screaming over the telephone, "They've been murdered! They've been murdered!" And then all sound ceased. Since the caller had not hung up the telephone, the police were able to trace the call. They hurried to reach the panic stricken caller.

All looked quiet and peaceful as the squad cars raced up the curving driveway of the palatial mansion that sat upon the hilltop overlooking the city.

The police rushed through the open front door and found the telephone caller sitting upon the floor, telephone receiver in hand. Her shock had been so great, that she sat in a deep stupor—neither hearing nor seeing the flurry of activity going on around her.

The hardened law officers were sickened by what they found within the rooms of the mansion—seven bodies, all beaten, stabbed, and strangled. Floors, walls, and even the ceilings were spattered with blood. One burly detective walked outside to hide his tears. He stood alone, sobbing.

No clues were found in the house to identify the murderers. Weeks went by with the police following up on hundreds of leads, but getting nowhere. The investigation had come to a standstill.

When all looked dark, a young detective remembered that while visiting his sister in the southwest, he met a man who talked about the miracles of Tele-Psychometry. He placed a hurried call to his sister. The man, Harold C., was on the next plane to the city where the murders had taken place.

When the police met Harold at the airport, they told him that they were going to drive him to a house where they wanted him to tell them of any *feelings* he might have. They told him nothing else.

As the party left the car and started walking toward the front door of the murder house, Harold stopped, as in disbelief.

"My God!" he cried, "I see bodies and blood all over the house. I can't believe it. My God, My God!"

Harold was so upset by the Tele-Psychometry vibrations he was receiving, that he first refused to enter the house. Without entering the house, Harold perfectly described the murder victims, how they were killed, and the rooms in which each body was discovered.

After finally entering the house, Harold gave the police physical descriptions of the men and women responsible for the murders, and the very unusual first names of two of the assailants. Harold later described a farmhouse, which he was seeing through his Sensory-Telemetry, and the geographical location of the isolated farm.

The law officers were awed by Harold's *Psychic Telemetry* performance, but made no comments to deny or confirm his Tele-Psychometry story. The next day, Harold returned to his hometown in the southwest.

In a matter of days, the mayor of the city announced to the press that suspects in the grisly murders had been arrested. Though he did not announce that the arrests were the results of Harold's miraculous powers, Harold had earned the eternal gratitude of a young detective, as well as the family and friends of the murder victims.

THERE IS MUCH MORE TO HAROLD'S STORY

Before being called upon to aid in solving the bizarre crime, Harold's life had not amounted to a great deal. He had many dreams, but did little to ensure their fulfillment. He was always half-sick—never feeling up-to-par. He never had enough money, nor a meaningful job. He was often heard to say, "I'm not *living,* I'm only existing!" In general, he described himself as just being plain miserable.

It was during one of Harold's low periods that a friend gave him a selection of pamphlets on the various aspects of *Psychic Telemetry*. Harold became very interested and studied the material. During this time, Harold was introduced to the visiting detective who would, at a later time, call upon him to help solve the mass-murder case.

Just three days prior to that significant telephone call, Harold decided he was going to change his life for the better—finally bringing his dreams into reality.

Harold took his pamplet on *Psychic Telemetry* (the same Enchantments you learned in Chapter Two), and pronounced with great force the Enchantments for:
1. Personal recognition.
2. Prosperity.
3. The opportunity to travel.
4. A loving wife and companion.

This is what the Magical Enchantments brought to Harold.

Harold's first Enchantment was for Personal Recognition. This he immediately received. He received personal recognition when that all-important telephone call was received from the distant city. He received great respect and esteem from the police department, his fellow peers, and the family and friends of the victims.

Harold's only desire was for personal recognition, not fame. But fame was his for the asking. As his *Psychic Telemetry* powers became more widely known, he found himself approached by reporters seeking interviews, and individuals and organizations seeking his help. Harold finally found it more convenient to move to a foreign country to escape the fame that would have undoubtedly been his.

Harold's second Enchantment called for prosperity. After the capture of the criminals, the family of the victims set up a special yearly annuity to be paid Harold so he would never have to work another day of his life.

The third Enchantment Harold declared was that he be presented the opportunity to travel. The magic of this Enchantment worked as positively as the others. Harold's first travel was the plane trip (his first) to the distant city—all at the expense of the Police Department. He then traveled to Scandinavia, where he finally moved permanently.

At last report, Harold is happily traveling to every major city in Europe.

After Harold's first three Enchantments were brought into reality, he said it was his fourth Enchantment that made his life "absolutely perfect." He wrote to tell friends of his new Swedish wife.

"It's like God made and moulded Ingrid especially for me."

THE POWER OF PSYCHIC-TELEMETRY CREATED EVEN MORE MIRACLES

This story has been one of miracles, but the miracles didn't stop with Harold.

Madge D. was the lady who made the original call to the police when the murders were discovered. She was the woman who was sitting on the floor in a stupor as the police arrived at the ghastly scene.

Madge was so horrified by what she had discovered, that she became a severely damaged woman, both mentally and emotionally. When ordinary methods of medical treatment failed, Madge was placed in an expensive, private, psychiatric hospital. The advanced treatment she received there was completely ineffectual. Madge's family had given up hope that she would ever recover.

In desperation, Madge's daughter attended a lecture on *Psychic Telemetry* Healing. After the lecture, the daughter appealed to the Healer to help her mother. And the Healer did!

Using the same techniques that you will learn in Chapter Seven, *Miracle Healing Through Psychic Medi-Telemetry,* the Healer had Madge returned to a complete state of normalcy within weeks. *Psychic Telemetry* succeeded where medical science had failed.

MAGIC WORDS THAT WILL INCREASE YOUR TELE-PSYCHOMETRY POWERS

Whenever you want to know the history of any place or thing, follow this very simple Ritual.

If you are divining the past of an object, gently place your hand upon it. If you want to divine a large object such as a house or other building, gently place your hand upon its various walls, repeating as often as necessary these Magical Words of Power:

"The vibration within the etheric memory of this (house, stone, ring, etc.) now speaks to me. My mind is now open, peaceful, and calm. I hear your story, I see your story, I feel your story. I will accept what is given me to know."

DEMITRIUS V. EARNS THOUSANDS OF DOLLARS FROM HER COLLECTION OF ANTIQUES

Demitrius was a middle-aged, lovely lady who adored antiques. Her home looked as if it were a beautiful reproduction of the Victorian past. Over the years, the lovely lady had spent every available cent to furnish her home with exquisite, priceless antiques. Priceless? Or so she believed.

As Demitrius had no insurance on her possessions, a friend suggested that she have her collection appraised, and purchase adequate insurance to cover any possible loss.

Demitrius was dumbstruck by the appraiser's report. She had been conned and swindled. Only a few items of her furniture were found to be authentic antiques. Most were cheap, worthless reproductions—not even worth insuring.

"I believed that people were honest," Demitrius told me. "How could so many people have cheated me? How could I have been so dumb?"

Demitrius' trusting nature had cost her a small fortune. What she believed to be wise investments in priceless objects from past decades, were actually valueless, or at best, worth a few hundred dollars at the most. Many people would have become embittered and pessimistic, if faced with a crisis the magnitude of the one faced by Demitrius. But not Demitrius.

It was not long after the appraiser reported the sad news to Demitrius, that I had the opportunity of visiting this fine lady. I found her to be determined to not only recover her monetary loss, but also to begin her own antique business, where she could deal with the public in an honest and efficient manner.

I met Demitrius again a few months later, and she related her activities of the previous months.

> "The first thing that I did after you visited with me, was to locate every individual I could who had sold me copies or duplicates of authentic antiques, or

those who had vastly overcharged me for legitimate pieces of merchandise. I couldn't locate all of the fraudulent salesmen, as some had moved. Some merchandise had been purchased so many years earlier, that I couldn't be sure as to where I had purchased the items—much of it had been through private parties.

"Except for one case, my threats of legal action fell on deaf ears. These charlatans had been very shrewd. They said that I didn't have enough proof of fraudulent intent to win any legal action. And they were right. This just gave me added determination to win my battle.

"I paid all of my 'friends' another visit. This time, I told them that if they didn't make financial restitution for their thievery, I was going to use psychic methods to disrupt their health, their business, and anything else they held sacred. They laughed, calling me 'crazy,' 'weirdo,' and 'sick.' I said, 'Okay, I gave you fair warning.'

"I used my Magic Tele-Aurascope, the Enchantments, and every other power I had learned in *Psychic Telemetry*. I really turned the whole works on them. It took awhile, and some of those con artists were pretty stubborn, but I received satisfactory restitution from every one of them. It'll be a long time before they cheat anyone again."

Demitrius went on to tell me of the fabulously successful antique business she had begun.

"Would you believe that I'm already making more money in a month than I did working at my previous job for a year? And I'm just getting started!"

I was curious, so I asked Demitrius how she knew she still wasn't being cheated when she purchased antiques for resale in her own shop? "Nothing to it," she replied. Demitrius explained:

"Before I purchase any item, I close my eyes and repeat the Tele-Psychometry Words of Power. Then I gently rub my hand over the object. When I begin to

Tele-Psychometry

see pictures of my Guardian Genie dressed in the fashions of the time period of the antique I'm considering, I know the piece is genuine. And I haven't been wrong yet!"

HOW INANIMATE OBJECTS "TALK" TO YOU

Just as Demitrius experienced visualizing periods in time by the dress fashion of her Genii, inanimate objects will talk to you in this same *Language of Symbols*—the Telemetric Sign Language you learned in Chapter Four.

The *Language of Symbols,* which is seen with your Visual-Telemetry, is not the only way inanimate objects "talk" to you. You may *hear* through your Audio-Telemetry, or you may *feel* through your Sensory-Telemetry. At other times, you will receive expressions through all three forms of Telemetry.

As you place your hand upon the thing you wish to psychometrize, repeat your Magic Tele-Psychometry Words. You immediately plug into the vibrations surrounding the object. This linkup stimulates your physical senses and manifests itself in Audio, Sensory, or Visual-Telemetry expression.

HOW TO "READ" THE PAST HISTORY OF ANY INANIMATE OBJECT

As you prepare to *divine* the history of any inanimate object, gently place your hand upon the object, and repeat the Tele-Psychometry Words of Power. If the object of your *divining* is small enough, you might prefer to clasp it gently, holding it in the palm of your hand.

Strange, but pleasant, sensations will overcome you as you begin your reading into the past. The object will begin "talking" to your Sensory, Audio, and Visual Telemetry Senses. The story will begin to unfold before you. The panorama of sensory experiences which unfolds before you is unique. At first appearance, your Tele-Psychometry story may seem to reveal itself in a piecemeal fashion. But this is not the case. Tele-Psychometry impressions come to you in a very logical manner.

At one time I agreed to undergo a test of my own powers of Tele-Psychometry. I did not know what object would be used for the test until I was handed a Catholic Rosary. I performed my Ritual, and commenced the "Reading."

> "I *hear* a foreign language.....I cannot speak the language, but I am sure that it is Italian. I *feel* that these beads were given to their owner as a gift—a recognition for much hard work that had been done. The rosary was a gift from a man of dignity and importance.
>
> "I *feel* myself drifting back through time—I am now at the turn of the century—the early 1900's. I see mountainous terrain, not too high, but more like rolling foothills. The vineyards and farmland which I see around me are very beautiful.
>
> "I *see* seven children, and I *hear* the name of Maria.
>
> "The lady who owned these beads was quite elderly and feeble when she died...I can *feel* my hand shaking, just as hers did as she held this same rosary. This wonderful woman did not die after a long or painful illness, she simply drifted peacefully into heaven during her sleep." (I *felt* myself doing this very thing—drifting peacefully up toward the clouds.)

The information given in this reading, while using my Tele-Psychometry powers, was confirmed at the end of the test. The rosary had belonged to a woman named *Maria,* who had been the mother of *seven children.* Maria was born in *Italy* among the *rolling hills,* where she grew up on her father's *farm* and *vineyard.*

The rosary was indeed a *gift.* Maria was devout. She worked so diligently among the poor, that in the *early 1900's* a Catholic cardinal presented the young girl with his own rosary as a token of his appreciation.

Through this very simple and logical manner, the history of the rosary was presented to me. I passed the "test" with flying colors—and you can do the exact same thing if you ever desire to.

Tele-Psychometry is accomplished very easily, and is a thoroughly delightful experience. It is easy and simple to do after you have performed your Ritual.

Most followers of *Psychic Telemetry* find Tele-Psychometry so fascinating, that they lay this book aside for several days. They just can't resist the excitement of *divining* the past from the many objects around them. You can do this same thing if you desire. The remainder of the *Psychic Telemetry* secrets will be waiting when you return to your book.

INANIMATE OBJECTS CAN BE POWERFUL FORCES FOR EVIL

Millions of people are unhappy and ill, but unable to discover the origin or basis of their misery. They resign themselves to lifelong acceptance of their sorrow.

Much, if not all, of the anguish suffered by these unfortunate souls can be removed if only they can become aware of the negative influence surrounding much of their physical environment. They are sensitive to and deeply affected by these forces of evil, of which they are totally unaware. This will never happen to you!

No life should be destroyed. You can be totally confident that after you finish this chapter, *you* will never again be influenced by an evil force surrounding any object within this entire universe. And Iris S. proved it.

IRIS S. REMOVED A CURSE FROM A HOUSE AND MADE $50,000 IN ONE YEAR

Jay and Karen were very happy in their medium-priced development home. They were so happy in their home, that they didn't want to cut their ties when Jay was transferred to another city. They decided to lease their dream home rather than sell it.

The neighbors were pleased as they watched the attractive new couple and their children move into the house. But time proved their attractiveness to be on the outside only.

In only a matter of days, the past history of the couple was unveiled. Their whole life together had been one of evil doing. The new couple were not married to each other, and had moved into the house with hopes of changing their identity. The woman had been released from prison five years earlier after serving a prison term for manslaughter. The male member of the couple had just been released from prison after serving a long jail sentence for armed robbery.

Only a few days after this couple had moved into the tidy home, the woman's legal husband was released from prison. He came to the home and shot holes through the front door, severely wounding his wife's lover. The evil force began to build its vibration around the entire house.

During the year that these people lived in the house, the man constantly beat the woman and children. The house was the scene of almost constant drunken orgies. The neighborhood was quite relieved when both the man and the woman were arrested for burglary, and removed from the neighborhood. But the house remained, cloaked in a vicious veil of evil.

With the house now empty, Jay and Karen returned on a vacation to paint and repair the home which held such fond memories for them. But something was different. The house did not seem to be the home that they had left one year earlier.

Whenever Karen entered the home to help Jay with the painting, she became moody and depressed. She was irritable, using every excuse to begin an argument with Jay. Finally, in disgust she walked from the house, swearing she would never enter it again. Before returning to their home in the other city, Jay and Karen put the house up for sale.

The very attractive house stood vacant for months while similar homes around it sold almost immediately.

The real estate lady who was handling the property at this particular time was a friend of mine. She told me that she didn't think she would ever sell the house.

"I drive up in front of the house with prospective buyers, and they're thrilled with it. I take them inside, and at least half the people have said, 'This is just what we've been looking for.' But before we get out of the house, they've changed their mind. Not one person has been able to tell me exactly why they suddenly change their opinion of the property. They say there is just something about the house that makes them nervous. No one wants to live in that house!"

In desperation, the price of the house was lowered to make it a bargain that was hard to resist. The house finally sold.

The couple who now bought the house were happily married with sons, aged eight and ten. Before one year had passed, the family was plagued by tragedy.

The wife had a near fatal accident; one son drowned while swimming in three feet of water; the second son developed epilepsy; finally, the husband deserted his wife for another woman.

The house was sold three times following these tragic events. The marriages of the next three owners ended in divorce. The house again stood vacant for months, until it was purchased by Iris, a widow with one small daughter.

IRIS BREAKS THE EVIL CURSE
UPON THE HOUSE

Iris had been told the history of the house before the purchase was made. "That house is selling for half the price of the identical homes around it. I can't afford to pass up a bargain like that," she told me.

Before moving into the house, and with no one else around, Iris performed the Ritual to Banish Evil Influences From Houses. She moved into her new home and was extremely happy. In fact, she had never been happier. It seemed like one good thing happened after another. Iris had certainly banished the evil influences from the once tragic-stricken home.

Iris had only lived in the house for a few months, when a Realtor knocked at the door.

> "I have a couple looking for a house in this neighborhood. They've driven by yours and have fallen in love with it. Would you be interested in selling it?"

Iris sold the house for a $30,000 profit. Now she wanted to increase her $30,000 windfall, but had no experience in stocks, bonds, or other investments. With her money in the bank, the happy lady now performed her Prosperity Rituals and Enchantments, and just sat back and waited. It didn't take long for the Enchantments to go to work.

Four days after Iris spoke the Enchantments, she received a telephone call from an old school chum, who told her, "For some reason, I just had the urge to call." During the course of their conversation, the chum mentioned that he was looking for a partner to purchase an old warehouse building. The plans were to renovate the old building and divide it into sections which would then be leased out to small speciality shops. Iris knew that this was the answer to her Prosperity Rituals, and joined her friend in the partnership.

The renovations on the old warehouse were going along nicely, when the representative of a large company offered to buy the building and complete the renovations. After some discussion, Iris and her partner decided to sell. Iris' profit? Another $20,000. In less than one year, Iris had earned $50,000.

At last report, Iris was building a new apartment complex. I have no doubt that Iris is now a millionaire—all because she used a simple Ritual to remove the evil vibrations from an inanimate object, a house.

THE POWERFUL RITUAL THAT WILL BANISH EVIL INFLUENCES FROM A HOUSE OR OTHER BUILDINGS

Before beginning your Ritual, relax, and with all the strength you possess, make this powerful Declaration.

"I am the ultimate Power of Good.

"I now banish from this house, and from the smallest blade of grass, all evil influences. All that will now remain within this house is the power that will bring wealth, health, and happiness to all who enter its doors. My Guardian Genie will bear witness to my exorcism. And so it is!"

When this powerful Ritual has been performed, you must then walk around the building three times counterclockwise while performing a second powerful Ritual. As you are walking around the house counterclockwise, continue repeating these words until your walk has been completed:

"I am now walking back in time. As I walk into the history of this home, I drive all influences of evil from its walls. It is only Good that remains. And so it is!"

This second Ritual can be very, very exhausting. After it has been completed, sit down and relax for just a few minutes, or until your strength has returned.

It would indeed be a very rare instance where an evil influence could withstand the two powerful Rituals which you have now performed. But if your Sensory-Telemetry warns you that an influence is still present, a small amount of investigation will reveal where the evil force is lurking.

Negative influences are attracted to negative shades of the color red. The vibrations from an evil past environment are the most difficult to detach and destroy if they are from these red tones. If an influence has escaped your Rituals, you will find that carpeting, wallpaper, or walls within the house are of these red tones.

If carpeting within the home is of a red tone, the evil influence can only be completely banished if the carpeting is taken up and removed from the premises. If the floor covering is to be replaced, yellow, gold, or blue should be considered as suitable substitutes.

Wallpaper, or other types of wall covering, must be completely stripped from the wall and replaced. Walls that have been painted with the negative color tones are much easier to correct. Simply wash the wall thoroughly (making sure that no areas are missed while scrubbing). Then paint the wall with a true white, good quality, paint.

Your complete exorcism of negative influences has now been successful. All that remains within the house or building are influences that will bring abundant joy to any person who resides within its walls.

THE CASE OF THE BLACK PENTACLE

An obviously distraught gentleman telephoned me one evening. "Do you believe in curses?" he asked. I assured him that I did. As we were talking, I began searching his home with my Visual-Telemetry.

"You don't have to tell me anymore. I can see a black object hanging on a wall over a bed. That's what's causing this sudden rash of bad luck," I told him. "Get rid of it, and your troubles are over!"

Forrest's son had apparently helped a neighbor clean the basement of an old apartment building. The young son had discovered a black pentacle among the many discarded items. He was attracted to the black, five-pointed star, took it home, and placed it on the wall of his bedroom.

Fortunately, the quick-thinking father used his common sense and immediately sought help as he felt the veil of negativity settle upon his home. His quick wit saved his family from a vibration that would have soon brought tragedy.

You can quickly remove all traces of the negativity which may cling to inanimate objects from your own home, and the homes of family, acquaintances, and friends. Your friends will soon be calling you the "miracle worker" as you bring health, wealth, and happiness into every home you enter. You will undoubtedly find that you do not have enough time to fulfill all the requests for exorcism which will come to you as your fame rapidly spreads.

RITUAL OF EXORCISM TO BANISH EVIL
FROM SMALL INANIMATE OBJECTS

This simple Ritual is guaranteed to work every time you use it. It's so simple, and yet so very powerful!

Tele-Psychometry

Place your hands firmly upon the object that you wish to exorcise, and repeat these Words of Power:

"In the Name of all that is Good, I now command that all evil influences leave this object now."

When this Ritual has been completed, an added Psychic Touch of Power is to cleanse the object in *chilled,* clean water.

HOW TO BUILD A POWER THAT ATTRACTS GOOD TO ANY INANIMATE OBJECT

You might term this Ritual, *How To Develop Your Own Lucky Charm.* The ancients wore various talismans because they knew the power of inanimate objects to ward off evil and draw good luck to the wearer. Lucky charms can be a ring, a horse shoe, or even an object as large, or larger, than an automobile. Wherever or whatever the object might be, you can be absolutely positive that vibrations of Good will shower upon it to draw every beneficial thing to you.

Again, place your hands firmly upon the object that you are about to make your *Magnet of Good,* and repeat very firmly and in a strong voice these magic words exactly seven times:

"I declare you a magnet of good!"

Then, cleanse the object in very warm water. If it is not practical to use water on the new lucky charm, place it in the warm sunlight for at least one hour.

You have undoubtedly already discovered, as have hundreds of people before you, that the beneficial uses of Tele-Psychometry are limitless. It would not be possible to write all of these benefits into one book, let alone in one chapter, as I have attempted to do.

YOU ARE NOW EQUIPPED TO CHANGE YOUR LIFE WITH TELE-PSYCHOMETRY

The power of Tele-Psychometry will now become more and more apparent. A day will never again pass that, in some manner, you will not use it to reap miraculous benefits.

You will never again be influenced by evil. Stand aside and allow a fountain of blessings to role gently over you as Tele-Psychometry goes to work.

Chapter Seven

Miracle Healing Through Psychic Medi-Telemetry

Whatever you are trying to heal, you know that the job will be done. You have already learned to call upon your dual Pillars of Power. Now you can add additional tools to your psychic powerhouse to perform healing miracles through *Psychic Medi-Telemetry*.

You are about to discover occult secrets of healing that are so powerful, that they have never been completely entrusted to students before this time. You will perform the same healing miracles attributed to the wise and ancient sages of the past.

HOW BERTHA P. CURED HER HUSBAND OF ALCOHOLISM

Bertha and Russ had been married for years when I first met them. Because of Russ' drinking problems, they were deeply in debt and faced foreclosure on their home. Russ had not held a steady job for months, and his physical condition steadily deteriorated. Russ was a nice guy, but he just didn't have the willpower needed to overcome his drinking problem.

"I've gone to A.A. and every other group I could join, but they just didn't help me," Russ said. "Once I even went to a sanitarium for treatment. I thought I was cured, but as soon as I got out, I hit the bottle again."

I asked Bertha and Russ to try the Porcelain Cup Treatment for one week. Both of them were doubtful that it could work, but in their desperation they agreed that anything was worth a try. Each night before going to bed, Bertha would perform her Porcelain Cup Ritual. Upon rising, Russ would drink from the cup. In four days I received a telephone call.

"Bob, this is Bertha. I just can't believe what's happening. Russ can't even smell alcohol without becoming deathly ill. He's tried to drink, but he just can't do it."

This is just an average case of Porcelain Cup Healing. It's been two years since Bertha's telephone call and Russ has lost all desire for alcohol. Russ is now a successful contractor. Russ and Bertha are not only happy and healthy, but on their way to making their first million dollars—all because of a simple, but powerful, porcelain cup.

HOW IDA CURED HER MOTHER'S SENILITY

Ida was a devoted daughter who took care of her mother since the death of her father. Ida had an excellent executive position with an advertising agency, and seemed to be living at the top of the world. Then Ida's world shattered.

Almost overnight, it seemed, Ida's mother began to show signs of senility. It was not long before Ida's mother was unable to stay alone. It was heartbreaking to both mother and daughter when the day came to place Clara in a convalescent hospital for the elderly.

"Bob, it seems so unfair. Mother's in perfect physical condition. Why did her mind have to go?"

I did my best to calm Ida. I told her that there was no need for Clara's condition to continue. I showed Ida the Porcelain Cup Ritual. She immediately felt a great power after performing the Ritual, and left immediately for the convalescent hospital. In less than a month, Clara was back in her daughter's home—fully capable of caring for herself.

Ida was bubbling over with joy when I joined her for one of the most delectable dinners of my life—all cooked by her 89-year-old mother, Clara.

Ida explained the miraculous porcelain cup cure.

"As soon as I left you, I went and bought the most beautiful porcelain cup I could find. I took it to the hospital, and in the privacy of mother's room, I performed the Ritual that you had shown me earlier. The next morning, on my way to work, I stopped and had mother drink the water from the cup. It was just like a miracle. In fact, the nurses did call it a miracle." Ida laughed when she went on to say, "Dr. Larsen can't explain the reversal of mother's senility. He said that there just wasn't any medical explanation." Clara stood and danced a little jig. "I can explain it, but I'll never tell!"

These are two simple cases of the effectiveness of your porcelain cup healing. Porcelain cup healing works to improve all conditions, but can only be described as miraculous in the treatment of alcoholism and diseases of the aged.

THE PORCELAIN CUP POWER RITUAL

It makes no difference as to the shape or size of your porcelain cup, but the cup must be constructed of true and unblemished porcelain. The vibration emitted by your perfect porcelain cup sends tentacles of power into the universe. These tentacles of power search until they discover the perfect chemicals necessary to invoke a healing. As the discovery is made, the healing potion is drawn back and placed in the porcelain cup by those invisible powers of heaven.

Before you begin your Power Ritual, fill your cup approximately two-thirds with water, and set it upon a table. Seat yourself before the cup, facing the east. Just as with the morning sun, it is from the east that all new light and power is born.

Your seating position should be with spine erect and feet placed firmly upon the floor. Close your eyes and visualize your

Pillars of Power, first on the right, then on the left. Cross your arms across your chest, placing your right hand on your left shoulder and your left hand on your right shoulder, invoking these Words of Power.

> **"I invoke the Spirit of spirits, that enters the darkened world with the morning sun, to fill me with the power of healing."**

Continue sitting passively for one or two minutes. Slowly remove your hands from the shoulders and hold them over the cup as Divine Healing falls from your hands into the water. Then place the cup of water on the nightstand, next to the bed where the person who needs healing will be sleeping. Immediately upon rising in the morning, the patient should drink all the contents of the miracle cup.

HOW HARVEY C.'S ASTHMA WAS CURED

Harvey C. was in his early twenties when I first met him at a healing lecture I was giving in southern California. After the auditorium had nearly cleared Harvey approached me about his problem.

"I think you're giving a lot of people false hope. I've had asthma all my life and no one's been able to cure it. The doctors help me to keep it under control, but they sure can't cure me!"

Harvey was a bitter young man. His life had been restricted because of his asthma. He felt that he had missed much from life, and didn't expect the future to be any better. Though deeply in love, Harvey refused to marry for fear that he would have children who would be handicapped with asthma as he had been.

Harvey's illness was a prime target for *gemstone healing*. I was so positive that Harvey's asthma could be cured, that I offered to lend him the topaz I had been using for demonstration purposes in my lectures. Then I showed Harvey the Gemstone Power Ritual. "I'll send your topaz back when I'm cured," he said in a mocking voice.

Harvey had completely slipped my mind. Several months later, I received a small package with a note inside.

"Dear Bob,
"I'm sorry that I kept your topaz so long, but I just can't believe all of the things that have happened to me since I attended your lecture.
"I have had no signs of asthma since I performed my first Gemstone Power Ritual. I no longer take medicine or visit doctors. I could never run more than a few steps until I was bent over, gasping for breath. Now I'm jogging and playing tennis with my beautiful wife—we were married last month.
"I now have my own topaz. It's been the best investment of my life."

PAUL P.'S EPILEPSY MIRACULOUSLY DISAPPEARED

Mrs. P. wrote to me, pleading for help for her 17-year-old, epileptic son, Paul. His heart's desire was to pursue a military career, which seemed only to be an impossible dream. The medicines prescribed by the doctors had helped Paul, but the drugs far from effected a cure for his disease.

I immediately wrote to Mrs. P., instructing her to purchase a small piece of jade and to follow the Gemstone Power Ritual which I had enclosed.

A year later, I received a post card from the eastern United States. It was from Paul.

"I've been accepted for Officer's Candidate School. Miracles really do happen."

THE GEMSTONE POWER RITUAL

As you begin your Power Ritual, choose the appropriate stone from the table which follows. Hold the stone in your right hand and repeat three times:

"The vibration of this stone increases in power and strength to heal and to bless."

If the stone is for your own healing, the next words should be a very loud, "I AM HEALED!" If the stone is to be given to another person, the words should be, "___(name)___ IS HEALED!"

Your Power Ritual is completed when you touch the stone to your abdomen, heart, and forehead. The stone must be carried on the person of the individual seeking the healing. It may be carried in a pocket, or made into a ring or necklace. The Gemstone Power Ritual should be repeated daily, until the miraculous healing through Psychic Medi-Telemetry is complete.

GEM	CURATIVE POWER
Emerald	An antidote for blood poisoning and gangrene, it is efficient in the healing of sores or wounds. The emerald will darken in color if the wearer is close to someone who wishes him harm. The gem will also darken in color if the wearer is in, or at, a place where negative or emotional turmoil has occurred.
Amethyst	Cures ulcers, nervous headache, and insomnia. This gem is noted for its calming effect upon the nerves. It soothes the temper and instills an inclination to forgive those who have wronged. The wearer will find new interests in cultural pursuits with an increase in social activities. The amethyst magnifies leadership qualities.
Ruby	Works to cure diseases of the liver and spleen. It can be an effective pain reliever if applied to the affected area of the body. Stops bleeding. The

wearer of the ruby will also have new interests and ideas regarding money-making schemes. The wearer will also find new interest from the opposite sex.

Turquoise — Effective in treating the loins, and pains of the chest that are not connected with the heart or lungs. The wearer of this gem will be more passive and less assertive. Revives new interest in, and from, the family. Wards off criticism.

Moonstone — Effective against all conditions of the lungs, including the common chest cold. The wearer will notice his reasoning powers are enhanced, and clear thinking induced.

Opal — Strengthens the memory and powers of perception. Should be worn during contract negotiations. The wearer will know the truth behind the statements of others.

Jade — Will strengthen the eyes. Controls epilepsy and disorders of the stomach. The wearer will become more self-assured and assertive.

Pearl — A lucky charm. It protects the wearer from surprise assaults, robberies, and accidents. The pearl draws love. Brings out the best in you.

Diamond — Cures heart disease, increases circulation, and heals gout. The wearer will become more courageous and outspoken. Increases the sex drive and controls the physical emotions.

Topaz   Heals burns, conditions of the nose, throat, and sinus. Effective in treating hay fever and asthma. The wearer of the topaz will want "time to be alone." Will feel a temporary need to withdraw from social activities.

Gem healing has been practiced for centuries, most recently by the ancient alchemists who jealously guarded their arcane secrets. Gem healing is no longer practiced by the rich and powerful only. Gem healing is a power that's yours—*now!*

Each area of the human body emits its own particular vibration, its own unique energy zone. When there is illness, the vibration becomes slower. The pulsating energy mass is reduced to irregular pulsations.

The gems in the preceeding table emit vibrations that compare to areas of the body when healthy. Your Power Ritual focuses the healing vibration to the affected area, raising the diseased area once again to perfection. Wearing or carrying your healing gem aids you in keeping your body whole and perfect.

GEM HEALING IS INEXPENSIVE

Bob F. went to the local "rock shop" to purchase an amethyst to cure his nervous headaches and insomnia. Bob happily found that he could purchase several uncut and unpolished gems for less than one dollar. Your healing gems need not be highly polished or of a precious nature, unless that is your personal desire. Stones *in the rough* are every bit as powerful as a brilliantly cut and polished diamond.

COLOR IS POWER

Scientifically, color is produced by vibrations. The number of light vibrations reflected by an object determines and produces its color. It is these reflected vibrations that you will harness and direct for healing. You will direct this laser beam of light to perform miracle healings hundreds of miles distant.

Color healing is another facet of your *Psychic Medi-Telemetry* healing powers. A force so powerful that it almost defies description.

EVELINA G.'S MIRACULOUS RECOVERY

Evelina's only hope was to find a suitable kidney donor when she first heard of Psychic Medi-Telemetry. Evelina had become so weakened by her kidney disorder, that it took two people to almost carry her to the hospital for her frequent treatments on the artificial kidney machine. Many times Evelina dipped close to death. She was a pathetic woman. There seemed to be little hope that Evelina would ever live a normal, healthy life. I became very busy and didn't follow up on Evelina's progress, though she remained very much in my thoughts.

While hiking on the trails at Mount Shasta, I heard a voice from below yell my name. I hesitated on the trail as I watched a young woman running quickly up the steep incline. It was Evelina. She was strong, healthy, and beautiful. Could this really be the young woman who just weeks before had been close to death, her body filled with poisons? Could this be the young woman who needed help to walk even a few paces? The same young woman who could not run up a mountainside? It was!

"I was so sick when I first read about the miracles of Psychic Medi-Telemetry, that I decided I'd rather be dead. No more medicines, no more machines, and no operation. I read about color healing, but I was too weak and mentally depressed to even try it.

"When things were the worst, I was lying in bed in a state of stupor. I heard beautiful music and the room seemed to fill with a blue mist. The mist became so thick, that I felt like I was being covered by an etheric blue blanket.

"Then my whole body began to tingle—it felt like little electric shocks were playing games at the small of my back. As suddenly as the mist arrived, it disappeared. I knew I was healed! I leapt from my bed and ran into the living room screaming, 'I'm healed, I'm healed!' Our house was filled with tears of joy that night."

I couldn't conceal my big grin as I watched Evelina briskly continue her hike up the mountain trail.

HAROLD F. SAW HIS LUNG CHANGE FROM DISEASE TO PERFECTION

Although Harold F. had no particular interest in *Psychic Telemetry,* he had no objection to his wife, Shirley, pursuing her interests. He was silently amused at the many minor miracles that kept occurring in their life. He silently believed that these miracles were as much due to chance as to any powers Shirley possessed.

Harold's face was ashen the day he returned from his annual physical. "Dr. Petersen says I have a spot on my right lung. He wants to operate next Tuesday morning," Harold said, his voice filled with fear.

Shirley immediately performed her Color Healing Ritual, and continued it daily until Harold checked into the hospital on Monday morning.

Monday was a day filled with agony and terror for Harold. X-ray after x-ray was taken in preparation for the operation that was to take place the next morning. Shirley was with Harold that evening when Dr. Petersen dropped by the hospital room.

"Harold, I don't know how to explain this. All of the tests we took today show no sign of the spot that was on your lung. Your lungs are perfectly clear. You can check out and go home tomorrow."

RITUAL TO PERFORM HEALING BY COLOR

Allow yourself at least ten minutes daily to perform miraculous healing by color. Go into a dimly lit room and sit comfortably in a straight-backed chair—hands resting upon the knees, palms upward. Breathe in deeply but slowly through the nose, exhaling rapidly through the mouth. This breathing exercise should be done three times. Sit quietly for a few moments until you feel completely relaxed. Then say:

Psychic Medi-Telemetry

"I invoke the Spirit of Healing to now make whole and perfect, ___(name)___."

You should then visualize a circle of color that corresponds to the organ you are about to heal. The healing has now begun. Now, within the circle of color, visualize the name of the person you are about to heal. Concentrate upon this name and the healing color as intently as possible for at least five minutes. As you begin to sense your Healing Ritual coming to a close, softly say:

"Praise God! ___(name)___ is healed!"

The Ritual of Color Healing is so powerful, that you might possibly feel tired and weakened as you bring the healing to a close. Don't be alarmed. Continue to sit relaxed for just a few minutes. All of your strength will quickly return.

COLOR HEALING TABLE

COLOR	CORRESPONDING ORGAN
Red	The heart and circulatory system
Steel	Gall bladder and the liver
Green	The spleen and pancreas
Yellow	The brain and nervous system
Pearl	The stomach
Blue	Kidneys
Purple	Lungs

THE POWER OF MAGNETIC HEALING

Until studying *Psychic Telemetry,* Louie A.'s life had been the eternal conflict that many feel—the false belief that a person cannot be rich and spiritual at the same time. Louie mistakenly believed that if he sought money, he would have to give up his desire of becoming a spiritual healer. If he chose to become a spiritual healer, he would have to become content to live in poverty. *Psychic Telemetry* proved to Louie that he could not only be a spiritual healer, but that he could become rich and famous as well.

At the time I met Louie, he was holding an executive position with one of Canada's largest electrical supply companies. Louie had a lovely wife and children, a well-paying job, and the respect of his community. But Louie was not happy—in fact, he was a miserable human being.

In August, I visited Louie and his family at their vacation retreat a few miles from Quebec.

"It's driving me crazy," he said. "I want to make a living for my wife and children, but I also want to devote my life to healing. I just know that I could be a powerful healer, but I can't give away all of my worldly possessions. That wouldn't be fair to my family."

I asked Louie why he couldn't be a healer and still have all of the money he needed and wanted. "It's easier for a camel to pass through the eye of a needle than for a rich man to get to Heaven," he said.

I explained to Louie that the false belief that one must be poor to be spiritual was a carryover from the Middle Ages. It just was not true. "Louie, this belief was cultivated by the rich to forestall revolution by the masses of the poor. If anything, it's unspiritual to be poor, not rich."

I then gave Louie some pamphlets with prosperity formulas and the varieties of healing that can be performed through Psychic Medi-Telemetry. Louie took to healing like a duck to water.

He performed the Power Ritual for Magnetic Healing, and left the house like a shot. Louie was back in fifteen minutes.

> "I thought I'd test my magnetic healing powers right away. Ken, next door, is confined to a wheelchair with arthritis. If anybody needs healing, it's him."
>
> The doorbell rang while Louie was still telling me about his healing experience. It was Ken.
>
> "I haven't been able to walk for months, and you got me out of my wheelchair. I walked over here by myself, and I want you to take this."
>
> It was a check for $500.

Louie has become a wealthy man since that August night. He has been called to every continent to heal those with "incurable" diseases. The money donations that he's accepted far exceed the salary he received from the electrical company. And you can do the very same thing.

AUDREY R.'S SPASTIC COLON CURED

Audrey R. was a victim of a very painful spastic colon. Her attacks had become so frequent, that she rarely left her home. Once active in civic organizations, Audrey had become a recluse. Audrey's husband, Jim, had to attend the many social functions required by his business—alone.

One day, Jim picked up a pamphlet on magnetic healing from his secretary's desk. He took the pamphlet into his office and read it thoroughly. That night, Jim performed his Power Ritual For Magnetic Healing, and placed his hands on Audrey's feet. Jim called me a few days later.

> "We went to the Opera Association's Black and White Ball last night. Audrey feels like a sixteen year old. She never missed a dance."

These healings are nothing unusual. By now you've read far enough into this chapter that you should be performing healings such as this on an almost daily basis.

POWER RITUAL FOR MAGNETIC HEALING

Sit quietly and passively until you begin to visualize your Pillars of Power. As the Pillars appear, repeat three times the affirmation:

> **"I am the Universal Magnet. I draw illness from those in pain and release this illness to the winds."**

Request your patient to remove his shoes and lie down. While your patient is in this prone position, you should grasp his feet tightly in your hands, knowing that you are drawing the poisons from his body. As you feel the negativity entering your hands, remove them from the feet and shake them violently. When the negativity has dropped from your hands, continue the treatment until you feel that the healing is complete. At the completion of the healing, wash your hands thoroughly with soap and water. This will ensure that no negative vibrations of the disease remain with you or attached to you in any way.

JACK T.'S EYESIGHT RETURNED AFTER RECEIVING HEALING FROM A GUARDIAN GENIE

Jack was playing first trombone in a popular band when he noticed that his eyesight began to fail. Within months, he was declared legally blind. Jack's life went from bad to worse. He lost his home and his friends. The bitterness he felt toward his affliction poured over into his personal life, until he drove his wife and family from him.

Jack was living in a Chicago skid row when a Psychic Telemetry Healer visited the cheap hotel in which he lived. He asked for a healing, but there were no noticeable results. There was something driving Jack from within. He knew that a Healing Genie could heal him. He tossed and turned throughout the night. He kept hearing a voice say, "Go to the Healer! Go to the Healer!"

Jack put on his clothes and asked the man on duty at the hotel desk to look up the address of the Healer. Without bus fare, blind and alone, Jack walked for miles across the streets of Chicago until he reached the Healer's home.

Jack made many trips across that city before his eyesight returned. But return it did. He now has his own band, and is a popular fund-raiser for the education of blind children. Also he is happily married to a wealthy socialite.

YOUR HEALING GENIE IS READY

You have contacted and talked with a Guardian Genie in previous chapters of this book. This familiar Genie will bring to you a Healing Genie. This Healing Genie will have but one responsibility—to work with you and through you to effect miracle cures upon the suffering and the lame. Your Healing Genie is just waiting for you to call. This Genie has the power to heal a withered limb or to return sight to the blind by working diligently to rebuild damaged tissue, cell by cell, regardless of how long it might take.

POWER RITUAL TO PERFORM GUARDIAN GENIE HEALING

Before beginning your healing treatment, clasp your hands as in a benediction, and repeat three times:

> "Divine Love, through me, blesses every nerve and cell, making ___(name)___ every bit whole."

You should then warn your patient that he will be feeling sensations of warmth and mild electric shocks. These are pleasurable experiences, but they can be unnerving to people who are not expecting these sensations of healing.

You should close your eyes and relax, asking that your Healing Genie draw close. As you recognize the approach, become even more passive. While in this state of passivity, you should allow your Healing Genie to direct and manipulate your hands. Let your hands move freely, without restraint. Your Genie knows what he is doing, and what needs to be done. The treatment is complete when your Healing Genie whispers a gentle "God Bless You," and withdraws.

DISTANCE IS NO OBSTACLE TO THE PSYCHIC TELEMETRY HEALER

As your fame as a Healer spreads, you will receive letters and long-distance telephone calls from around the world—all asking for your intercession. *You* can't be everywhere, but your *Healing Genie* can!

POWER RITUAL TO PERFORM HEALINGS AT A DISTANCE

Sit erectly upon a chair in a dimly lit room. Relax and visualize your Pillars of Power. Call your Healing Genie to you. He will stand directly before you, between your Pillars of Power. *Always* thank your Genie for coming.

Take your written messages and read to your Genie the names and addresses of those who require healing. As your Genie withdraws, close your eyes and remain completely passive until your Healing Genie returns to tell you that the healing has been completed.

You have participated in a very powerful Healing Ritual, and you might feel a bit giddy when your Genie returns. Become fully alert and remain seated for a minute or two. The giddiness will be short-lived. You will be filled with such awe-inspiring power, that you will feel as if you're floating on a cloud—a beautiful experience indeed.

THERE ARE SOME PEOPLE WHO CANNOT BE HEALED

You will rarely find a person who cannot be healed, but you will meet a few. This failure to heal does not reflect upon your Psychic Medi-Telemetry healing powers.

There are certain individuals who actively reject any healing attempts by occult methods. Their stubbornness and disbelief builds a wall of negativity around them which repulses honest attempts to relieve their suffering. Healing only goes to those who want it and accept it. Don't waste your time or energy on people who do not want your help. Let their problems remain their problems.

WHY AN ILLNESS RETURNS

While practicing your healing endeavors, you will discover a unique group of people who have had complete cures, yet their illness returns.

There is always a *cause* for an illness. If the cause of an illness has not been removed, the illness will return. This is exactly what happened to Betty.

Betty C. was suffering from an acute lung condition caused by heavy cigarette smoking. A practitioner of the art of healing via Psychic Medi-Telemetry cured her lung condition, but cautioned her that she must give up cigarettes. A medical doctor confirmed Betty's cure.

Betty was elated over her cure, but she ignored the healer's warning and returned to heavy cigarette smoking. Within weeks her condition had returned.

POWER RITUAL FOR DIAGNOSING THE ORIGIN OF A DISEASE

Lie down in a darkened room with your arms resting beside your body (your arms, ankles, legs, or feet should not be crossed in any manner). There should be no pillow under your head.

Repeat three times the affirmation:

"I peer into the Universe to discover the cause of (name)   illness. The Truth comes to me now!"

When your affirmation has been completed, become passive and gaze gently at the ceiling of the room. Within minutes, writing will appear on the ceiling, giving you a complete diagnosis of the problem. Sit up slowly and remain seated for a few moments before you resume your normal activities.

THOUGHTS CAN CAUSE AN ILLNESS

Psychic Telemetry has already proven to you that thoughts are very real things. Thoughts can bring us our blessings, but they can also bring us our curses.

There are general correlations between negative thought patterns and broad groups of major physical complaints. The following table is furnished as a general guide to use with your Psychic Medi-Telemetry healing powers.

THOUGHT PATTERN		ILLNESS
Hatred, pessimism	=	cancer
Greed, selfishness	=	high blood pressure, strokes
Frustration	=	respiratory ailments, throat and sinus problems
Inferiority	=	skin rash, boils, arthritis
Impatience	=	ulcers, heart trouble, migraine headaches
Fear, guilt	=	diseases of the nerves, spinal ailments

There you have them: four powerhouses of healing energy. Never again do you, your family, or your friends need to experience illness or pain. You are forever free of the annoyance caused by a diseased or imperfect physical body.

Chapter Eight

How to Use Psychic Astral-Telemetry for Getting Anywhere or Reaching Anybody

Psychic Telemetry allows you to become an invisible traveler to anywhere in the world. You can listen to conversations and you can see what's going on, completely undetected.

Using the instructions in this chapter, you can benefit yourself by influencing the thoughts of others, while accumulating knowledge previously held as secret.

**IN THE WORDS OF ST. PAUL,
"IF THERE IS SUCH A THING AS AN
ANIMAL BODY, THERE IS ALSO A SPIRITUAL BODY"**

St. Paul recognized that there were two bodies in man, but people believed in various forms of this dualism for hundreds, even thousands of years before St. Paul wrote his Letters to the early Christians.

You already have this power to separate your spiritual body from your physical body. And while separated, your conscious mind will remain with your spiritual body as you invisibly travel the world over.

HOW YOU WILL FEEL AS YOUR TWO BODIES SEPARATE

You will feel the best you've ever felt in your entire life, as your two bodies separate and you begin your first Astral-Telemetry flight. Everything appears to be absolutely beautiful. The first thing that you will probably notice is that your spiritual body is just as real to you as your physical body ever was.

Your second experience can be a cause of hilarity or of gentle concern, though most people do find it amusing. Many find it to be humorous as they stand looking at their physical bodies, which are lying in slumber—then learning that physical objects are the things that are no longer real.

One of my students was recently telling me of the sensations she experienced during her first Astral-Telemetry projection.

> "I did nothing but laugh during my first Astral-Telemetry experience. I guess I should have been concerned, but I found everything to be very amusing.
>
> "What started me giggling right away was how funny I looked lying upon the bed, sound asleep. I should say not how funny I looked, but how funny my body looked.
>
> "Then I decided to open the bedroom door and walk into the hall. Then I really laughed. I kept reaching for the door knob, but my hands would go right through everything that I tried to touch! All of the things that had always been *real* to me, were the things that were now *unreal*.
>
> "It was just a fantastic feeling when I found that I didn't have to open doors to pass to the next room. I walked right through the door like it didn't even exist."

Though your reactions may be slightly different than the lady's above, you will experience this same ability to walk through walls and doors. Nothing can be kept secret from you—there is no longer such a thing as a locked door. You can enter any place at will. You can think of a place, or a person, and you are instantly there. You can be in America one minute, and in Bombay, India, the next. You can travel from Africa to Australia faster than the wink of an eye.

ASTRAL-TELEMETRY EXPERIENCES ARE NOT UNCOMMON

All out-of-the-body experiences are induced from a state of unconsciousness. This unconsciousness can be caused by an anesthetic, natural sleep, a hypnotic trance, traumatic shock, or as a result of an accident.

Occult books and periodicals are filled with the personal experiences of people involved in accidents who have blacked out just before impact. And after the impact, they find themselves observing the whole accident scene as their body lies unconscious upon the ground.

A youngster of eleven recently told me of his own Astral-Telemetry experience that was induced as the result of an accident. The youngster apparently lost control of his bicycle as he was riding down a very steep hill. He remembered being thrown into the air, but he suddenly found himself floating high above the ground. He saw his body hit the ground and remain motionless. He had no feeling of fear, and he felt no pain from the fall.

While still floating in the air, he watched two ladies run from a distance to where his body lay sprawled on the ground. He heard their conversation and watched their movements as they attempted to revive his body from its unconscious state. Then, as suddenly as he had left his body, he returned to it—fully conscious and aware of the pain from his broken shoulder.

Many other people write about the very common experience of their spiritual body separating from their physical body as the result of an anesthetic. It almost seems the norm as these individuals watch, fully conscious in their spiritual bodies, as the doctors operate upon their unconscious physical bodies.

Obviously it is not practical, nor is it desirable, to accomplish an out-of-the-body experience as the result of an accident, anesthetic, or a traumatic experience. Astral-Telemetry will reveal a safe and foolproof method of inducing the separation of your spiritual body from its physical counterpart.

HOW ASTRAL-TELEMETRY MOVED REVEREND E. FROM A STOREFRONT CHURCH TO A $125,000 SANCTUARY

Reverend E. was leading a very active, but financially poor, storefront church in one of Long Beach, California's less-than-desirable neighborhoods. Disaster loomed on the horizon, as the little church was given 30 days to vacate the premises while an Urban Renewal Project prepared to level the entire neighborhood.

Three weeks passed, and the church still had no new building to move to. Then Reverend E. determined that he was going to have to do more than pray if he was going to keep the church doors open. The good paster was unsure whether the Astral-Telemetry Ritual would even work, as he lay down on his bed and recited its words. But the Ritual did work. He instantly found himself floating in the air above his unconscious physical body. "What a wonderful feeling that was," he later confided to a friend.

However, there was work to do, and Reverend E. quickly went about his task. Silently and unobservedly, he glided up and down the streets of the city. He noticed a group of vacant buildings on a corner in what he had previously thought to be a neighborhood whose zoning ordinances had prohibited the construction of commercial property.

"I was intrigued by the group of buildings, and just had a hunch that I had found the right place," Reverend E. told me. "I knew that unless a miracle occurred, there was no way that my church could afford to purchase the property. But a miracle did occur.

"As I was astrally investigating the buildings, two men, who I later learned were business partners, drove up and entered a small office in the largest of the buildings."

Completely invisible, Reverend E. stood in a corner of the office and listened to the conversation between the owners of the property. He didn't like eavesdropping on a private conversation, but believed that the circumstances of the moment merited the intrusion.

He discovered that the buildings were deliberately kept vacant, as they permitted a large tax write-off for the business partners. Though the buildings were advertised for sale, their sale price was $50,000 over their fair market value—ensuring that they would not only remain vacant, but would remain a lucrative tax write-off as well.

Reverend E. saw the potential of the property. The one large building would be sufficient not only for a sanctuary, but for Sunday school rooms, a large kitchen, and a social hall, as well. The three remaining smaller buildings could be leased to small businesses. But how could he acquire this magnificent piece of property?

"I thought about nothing but that piece of property the entire next day," the Reverend related. "There had to be a way of acquiring it that would be mutually advantageous to the church as well as the owners."

That same night, Reverend E. astrally visited one of the property owners as he lay sleeping.

"I entered the man's bedroom and saw him fast asleep. I leaned over and whispered in his ear that a minister would visit him the next day to discuss the property in question. I emphasized that he would think of a way to save a great many tax dollars by selling the property to the minister."

The Reverend visited the partner's office the next morning, asking to speak to the man he had astrally visited the evening before.

"You'll never believe this," the partner said, "but I dreamed last night that a minister was going to inquire about that property. I just can't believe the coincidence," he said.

The minister explained that his church had no money to make a down payment on the property, but could easily make any monthly payments by leasing out the three detached buildings.

"I know that you are asking $175,000 for the property, but I would be willing to pay only what it's worth."

"What is it really worth," the partner asked?

"It has a market value of $125,000, but you could sell it to my church for much less, and count the difference as a church donation. That could save you a lot of money on taxes," Reverend E. explained.

"I can see you're really a business man," the surprised partner said. "How in the world did you find all of that information?"

The minister chuckled as he said, "God tells us a lot of things when we listen to Him."

The purchase of the church property was quickly concluded. It was truly a miracle. The partners lowered the price of the property to $100,000—$25,000 below its fair market price. They then donated another $25,000 to the church. The church then used this $25,000 to make a down payment on the property. But the partners didn't stop there.

There was still the challenge of leasing the three smaller buildings so that there would be sufficient income to make the loan payment. Within days, the man Reverend E. had astrally visited during sleep found lessors for all three buildings—a chiropractor, a children's nursery school, and a mail-order cosmetic business. The rents from these leases were sufficient to not only make the church loan payment, but to pay Reverend E. a monthly salary as well.

Miraculously, almost overnight, a little storefront church in the wrong part of town became a thriving, prosperous, metropolitan religious center.

It really wasn't a miracle. It only appeared as a miracle to those people unfamiliar with the ease by which the impossible become the possible when one influences the course of events through Astral-Telemetry.

HOW TO INFLUENCE THE THOUGHTS
OF OTHERS THROUGH ASTRAL-TELEMETRY

You can easily and dramatically influence the thoughts of others in much the same way as did Reverend E. in the case history you have just read.

The ideal moment to influence the thoughts of another person is when he or she is in a sleeping state. When their conscious mind is asleep, you are free to speak directly to their subconscious mind. Your voice to the subconscious is remembered upon awakening, but the person believes that it was a dream. They have no conscious recollection of your nocturnal visit.

It is slightly more difficult to influence the thoughts of an individual when they are in a wakened condition. The conscious mind moves so rapidly, that there is little opportunity to inject an external thought. But it can be done, and here is how you do it.

After you have completed your Astral-Telemetry Ritual, project yourself to the person whose thoughts you are going to influence. Stand as close to the individual as possible, and wait for the moment that they relax a bit. As they remain relaxed, concentrate on the thought that you want to place within their mind. When the thought has been placed, let nature take its course. Return to your own sleeping body and relax. You can be confident that the thought you placed within the mind is being mulled over and acted upon.

HOW ROSE K. WON A LEGAL ACTION WORTH
ALMOST $30,000 WHEN SHE LEARNED
THAT A MAN HAD INTENTIONALLY KILLED HER PET DOG

Rose K. was a lonely widow whose greatest comfort and best friend was a little black mongrel dog that had mysteriously appeared at her door almost ten years before.

When Rose heard little Pete barking at the fence in the backyard, she paid scant attention. He often barked through the fence at the neighbors. When his barking ceased abruptly, she went to investigate. She found Pete lying unconscious upon the ground, his legs were twitching uncontrollably. Near hysteria, Rose picked up the black bundle of curly hair and rushed him to the veterinarian.

Pete was dead when Rose arrived at the animal hospital. She wanted to know what had happened to her little friend. "Something hit him and crushed his skull," the veterinarian told Rose.

Rose, now terribly upset, returned home and lay down to rest and think. She later told me that she just could not understand what had happened to her dog.

While lying on the bed, emotionally drained, Rose decided to use Astral-Telemetry to invisibly visit her neighbor. She had no reason to suspect that he was instrumental in Pete's death, but maybe he could provide a clue.

"I glided quietly into my neighbor's living room, just in time to hear him tell his wife that he had finally put an end to that darned dog's barking next door. I stood listening in disbelief as he described how he had leaned over the fence and hit Pete as hard as he could with a large piece of lumber," she told me.

Rose concluded her Astral-Telemetry visit and returned to her sleeping body. Later that evening she went next door and accused her neighbor of willfully killing her little friend, Pete.

"I don't know what you're talking about," the neighbor said. "I didn't even touch your dog, let alone kill him. I think you're crazy, lady."

Thoroughly enraged, Rose was quick to consult an attorney.

"I had no proof that my neighbor had killed Pete, and I couldn't find a lawyer who would take my case without proof," she confided.

Rose returned home and performed her Astral-Telemetry Ritual. She scoured her neighbor's yard from one end to the other. She was unsuccessful in locating the piece of lumber that was used to kill Pete.

"There was only one other place to look," she said, "and that was in the house. Finally, in the closet of the master bedroom, I found a large board with Pete's black hair stuck to it. I found the board, but I still needed the help of an attorney.

"I had earlier talked to a sympathetic attorney who would gladly help me if I had one iota of proof of my neighbor's guilt. I astrally traveled to his office, and luckily found him in a relaxed mood. I concentrated on my problem, and placed the thought in his mind that he should telephone me."

The lawyer did telephone Rose. She was so convincing in telling her story of her neighbor's guilt, that the lawyer asked Rose to meet him at the district attorney's office.

"My attorney advised me to lodge a formal complaint against my neighbor, which I did. The district attorney then informed the man that he was charged with a felony—cruelty to animals.

"Before this criminal case came before the municipal court, my attorney, acting in my behalf, filed a personal legal action against the man for $100,000 as compensation for the loss of my dog."

As is usual in legal cases of this magnitude, the opposing attorneys bring together the parties involved in an attempt to settle the case before a long and costly trial.

"My neighbor's attorney, who was a representative of his insurance company, insisted that there was not one bit of proof that my neighbor was guilty of my charges, and that they were not going to pay me one red cent. In fact, they considered suing me for harassment.

" 'Just a minute,' I said. 'The board that man used to kill my dog is hidden in the closet of his master bedroom this very minute!' "

Rose's neighbor first gasped, and then he completely broke down, admitting his guilt to both attorneys.

Rose didn't have to go to court. She accepted the $28,000 settlement offered by the insurance company. With his guilt already established, the man who had wielded the destructive board meekly accepted the three-month jail sentence imposed by the Municipal court judge.

Neither the money nor the jail sentence brought little Pete back to Rose, but, in her words, "there was a great deal of satisfaction in seeing justice done."

ASTRAL-TELEMETRY IS HARMLESS

Astral-Telemetry is a very enjoyable experience without the slightest element of danger. Contrary to what you may have read or heard, Astral-Telemetry is a totally safe method to accomplish an out-of-the-body experience.

Some writers who have mastered Astral-Telemetry claim that they have had unpleasant experiences while away from their physical bodies. But their unpleasant experiences are rather silly when you analyze them.

One writer turned against Astral-Telemetry because he became terrified during an astral journey. "I almost died of fright," he wrote. I admit that on the surface, "almost dying of fright," does seem to be a legitimate complaint against astral travel. But the writer of that fearsome statement failed to tell you why he was really frightened, as do other opponents of Astral-Telemetry. What frightened that individual was really quite silly.

Having heard of riots that were occurring in a European country, the gentleman in question decided that he would astral travel to Europe to see the riots first-hand. He projected his spiritual body to Europe quickly and smoothly. He became terrified when he found himself right in the middle of a riot. He quickly forgot that no harm could come to his spiritual body, which was immune to all physical forces. If he was going to become frightened, he had no business projecting himself to the riot area in the first place.

When you know the whole story, the objections to Astral-Telemetry are petty and frivolous. Astral-Telemetry can be one of your most fulfilling psychic endeavors.

You need not have the slightest fear that there will ever be difficulty in re-entering your sleeping body. If anything does disturb your reposing body at home, you will return to it instantly, and wake as easily as from a restful night's slumber.

HOW DELBERT L. PASSED A VITAL CIVIL SERVICE EXAMINATION BY USING ASTRAL-TELEMETRY

Delbert L. held the lowest position in the county treasurer's office, and he was about to take a civil service examination that would make every difference in the poverty-stricken life-style that he was now living.

Delbert lived in a cramped apartment with his aging parents.

"Mom and Dad can't work, and their welfare check doesn't even furnish them with the necessities," Delbert explained. "My salary is just enough to furnish us with the food we need. There isn't a cent left for luxuries.

"It's been years since I've bought a new suit, and I'd sure like to buy a television set for Mom and Dad. The apartment gets pretty lonely for them while I'm at work."

Delbert studied hard for the examination. He studied until his eyes ached.

"One night I was escaping the pressures of the moment by using Astral-Telemetry to travel to a beautiful park on the other side of town. When I started to return home, I suddenly found myself in a county supervisor's office, where the examination to be given the next day was being stored.

"At first my conscience wouldn't let me look at the test questions, but 'darn it,' I said, 'anyone else who works with Astral-Telemetry can do the same thing!"

"I studied the test questions until I had them firmly in my mind, then I spent the rest of the night looking up the answers."

Not surprisingly, Delbert passed the civil service exam with flying colors.

"My parents have a television set now, and a few other luxuries," Delbert said. "I don't feel that I did anything wrong. What I did wasn't for myself, it was to help others. Only good came from it."

HOW TO USE ASTRAL-TELEMETRY TO ACCOMPLISH AN OUT-OF-THE-BODY EXPERIENCE

Astral-Telemetry will lift you very simply and comfortably into your first out-of-the-body experience. There are simple exercises that will help you to travel anywhere your heart desires.

First, sit in your usual chair in a dimly lit room and perform your Pillars of Power Ritual. Gaze at the Pillar on the right, then to the Pillar of light on the left, and to your Guardian Genie. When you are completely relaxed, ask your Genie to aid you in your Astral-Telemetry exercises.

When your Genie has been contacted, repeat this Enchantment:

> "I will now enter the astral domain. I will travel freely and unrestricted to any place that I desire.
>
> "I am safe and secure in all of my efforts. My spiritual body will now drift free of its physical counterpart. And so it is!"

Relax for a few moments, then calmly walk to your bed and lie down. Lie flat on your back with your hands at your side, eyes closed.

Now remember how you felt as you were sitting in the chair performing your Rituals. Imagine your Genie beckoning to you as he stands between your Pillars of Power in another room. Now imagine that you are sitting up. Then pretend that you have placed your feet upon the floor. Now imagine yourself walking across the room toward your Ritual Chair and your Magic Genie. It doesn't matter that you aren't physically moving. Just pretend that you are.

Practice this exercise for approximately ten minutes a day, and you will soon discover that you are no longer pretending. You will feel the floor under your feet as you walk toward your chair, your Genie, and your Pillars of Power.

How to Use Psychic Astral-Telemetry

Look at the bed! Sure enough, you will see your physical body fast asleep. Don't become startled, or you'll zip right back into your body and wake it up from its peaceful sleep.

Keep your first astral journeys close to home. Get used to the feeling of being free of your physical body before you travel to unfamiliar surroundings.

When you are at ease with your new found power, travel to wherever you wish—listening and watching those things that will help you along your Psychic-Telemetry road to abundant riches.

HOW TONY R. TRAVELED INVISIBLY FROM GUAM TO SAN DIEGO AND PROVED THAT HIS WIFE WAS DECEIVING HIM

Tony R., a petty officer in the navy stationed on Guam, was sure that his wife whom he left in San Diego was being unfaithful to him. Her letters were full of warmth, but Tony still had his doubts.

"She seemed to make too many excuses for not coming to visit me in Guam. First she was ill. Then she had to wait while she trained a new girl for her job. And then she wrote that her parents were visiting for a month. It was one excuse after another," Tony recounted. "So one evening I was just plain fed up. I lay down on my bed and used my Astral-Telemetry to visit her in San Diego.

"I drifted into her apartment through the closed door and found my best friend sitting in my favorite chair. He acted very much at home."

Tony became furious as he watched his wife walk from the bedroom and sit on the man's lap. He was enraged as he watched her passionately kiss her lover.

Tony watched as she reached over and lifted her government allotment check from the table.

"You'd better cash this tomorrow, honey," she said. "I wonder what Tony would think if he knew he was paying for his best friend's new car?" she laughingly said.

Tony swung his arms wildly as he tried to hit his friend. "Neither of you will be laughing the next time I see you," Tony screamed.

Tony applied for a leave the very next day, and was on the first navy plane headed for San Diego.

"My wife opened the door of her apartment and flew into my arms," Tony said.

Tony sat his wife down and confronted her with what he knew.

"First she flew into a rage, and then she cried. She accused me of listening to gossip.

"I divorced her, of course, and found myself a woman who is faithful. I know that she's faithful because when I'm away, I'm forever using Astral-Telemetry to travel invisibly in and out of our apartment."

HOW YOU WILL FEEL DURING YOUR FIRST ASTRAL JOURNEY

I want to emphasize that you will feel absolutely wonderful during your astral journeys. It is invigorating and restoring. One important difference which you will notice is that you cannot pick up, or move, physical objects—which I have previously mentioned in this chapter.

Many people expect Astral-Telemetry adventures to be similar to those experienced from a dream state. However there are few comparisons between an out-of-the-body experience and a dream.

In a dream experience, your subconscious mind pumps images into your conscious mind while you lie sleeping. There is no separation of the spiritual body from the physical body, as is true in Astral-Telemetry.

When your two bodies separate during Astral-Telemetry, your consciousness travels with your spiritual body. You can hear and see exactly as if you were in your physical body, but no one can see, hear, or touch you. And unlike a dream where the memory is sometimes fuzzy, Astral-Telemetry experiences are clear and sharp within the mind. Just as clear as anything you might experience in your physical body.

You do not lose any of your Psychic-Telemetry abilities while on your astral journeys. If you wish, you can perform any of your Rituals or Enchantments while you are out of your physical body. They are effective whenever they are performed.

HOW HARRIET O. PERFORMED AN ASTRAL RITUAL TO GAIN THE LOVE OF A MAN

Harriet O. is an advanced Psychic-Telemetry student who regularly combines Enchantments and Rituals with her Astral-Telemetry. I recently heard her describe how she had won her husband.

"Jeff is an extremely handsome man, and every single woman in town was trying to wangle a date with him. And aside from being handsome, he was rich. He was being invited to the best parties, and was surrounded with luxury wherever he went. He was enjoying his life, and I can't say I really blamed him. But I swore that I was going to make myself so desirable, that Jeff would lose his interest in everyone else but me—and I never had a date with him yet."

Harriet used Astral-Telemetry several times to secretly visit Jeff in his apartment. During one of these visits, she performed the Enchantment to make herself desirable.

"It gave me a thrill to be beside Jeff, even though he wasn't aware that I was there. I think that being close to him gave the Enchantment more power.

"It startled me a bit to see Jeff strip down to do his exercises. I sat in a chair and watched Jeff. He was the most desirable man I had ever seen.

"Just as he was finishing his exercises, I repeated the Enchantment to make myself desirous. I knew that the Enchantment had worked when Jeff looked in the telephone book and wrote my number on a pad. I quickly returned to my body. I knew that I'd be hearing from Jeff soon."

Harriet had just enough time to stand up and relax for a few minutes before the telephone rang. It was Jeff.

"I hope you'll excuse me for calling so late," Jeff said. "I just haven't been able to get you off of my mind. Will you have dinner with me tomorrow evening?"

Harriet was the envy of all her friends when she and Jeff walked into the country club for dinner.

"You should have seen all of those jealous eyes staring as Jeff catered to my every whim. It was obvious to everyone that Jeff was trying to control the passion he was feeling toward me.

"Even Jeff couldn't understand why he had developed such an uncontrollable passion for me. I knew why, and naturally I took full advantage of the situation."

From then on, everything went Harriet's way. Her wedding to Jeff was the high point of the social season. She now enjoys her luxury auto as she travels between her luxurious home and the beach cottage that Jeff gave her as a wedding gift.

"Before I married Jeff, I had to watch every penny that I spent. But it's a lot different now. Jeff criticizes me because I don't spend enough money on myself—but there isn't anything else to buy. I already have every material possession that I ever dreamed of.

"Jeff married me willingly, and he never even glances at another woman. All of his previous girlfriends wonder how I ever landed him. When I moved in with my Astral-Telemetry Enchantment, they didn't know what hit him."

YOU CAN NOW GO ANYWHERE AND REACH ANYBODY

Practice your Astral-Telemetry. Like any other Psychic Telemetry ability, it might take a few attempts before you are successful. But after the first successful effort, there's nothing to hold you back.

You no longer need to have pressing questions about others in your mind. You can secretly and invisibly watch their every move and hear their every word.

Astral-Telemetry is not only fun, it is an ability that can open an entirely new life for you. A life of riches, good health, and love.

Chapter Nine

Psychic Telemetry Games That Will Make You a Winner Every Time

This chapter can be one of the most important in this book. One feature of *Psychic Telemetry* is that there are innumerable ways that you can manipulate forces that command miracles to happen for you. You will now learn to focus this force through psychic games.

Your entire environment can be changed by this practical method of *Psychic Telemetry*. These psychic games can be used to produce the same Power that you have discovered in other *Psychic Telemetry* chapters. These games can be used for entertainment at parties and among friends. Though these games are popular as an evening's enjoyment, they will be secretly revealing to you the psychic power, the true personality, the health, and the wealth of its players.

Not only will these games reveal the deepest held secrets of the players, they will afford you the opportunity to practice your *Psychic Telemetry* skills completely undetected by those around you.

I will first show you how to use these powerful forces as a game that will reveal the secrets of the game's players exclusively to you. Secondly, I will teach you to use these same games as powerful Rituals to control others, influencing their every thought and action.

Refinements of these psychic games involve the invoking of Enchantments, Positive Declarations, Symbols, Colors, or Rituals. They are designed to give you unprecedented power to control those individuals surrounding you. These games will give you the feeling of a force pouring through your body, which is seldom experienced in this Aquarian Age. It is a force that was so adroitly manipulated by the Ancient Mystics, that it has remained undiscovered by most seers and sages of the modern day.

I will present all of this in a simple step-by-step form. You are on the road leading to miraculous magic as you acquire money, love, power, success, happiness, and contentment.

HOW PSYCHIC GAME ONE REVEALED THAT CLAUDIA F.'S HUSBAND WAS UNFAITHFUL

Claudia F. and her husband, Ralph, belonged to a very active social group. The group met at a different home each month, where it was the obligation of the host and hostess to plan entertaining activities, as well as provide food and liquid refreshment. When it became Claudia's turn to entertain, she decided that she would play psychic games.

Claudia had noticed that during the past several months, Ralph had become less attentive than usual. And though she had no proof of any wrongdoing, her suspicions were aroused when it became necessary for her husband to spend more and more evenings working late at the office.

Ralph had always been a good husband, but Claudia couldn't believe what she was seeing as she analyzed his aura each day.

"I kept seeing this dark crimson color in Ralph's aura," she wrote to me. "I thought that I was becoming overly emotional, and I didn't trust my aural observations."

Claudia went on to explain how she used Psychic Game One to prove Ralph's infidelity.

"The first game, which I decided to play on the night we entertained our social group, was pulling colored marbles from a paper bag. I offered small prizes to the persons who could pull the most marbles of the same color from the bag.

"I had been instructed at a *Psychic Telemetry* class that this marble game was an ideal method to secretly discover personality characteristics of the players. I didn't know until the night of my party how well the game really works!"

Claudia's suspicions of her husband's wandering eye were confirmed when, time after time, he drew a dark crimson-colored marble from the bag.

"I knew my aural colors perfectly. There was no question that Ralph's repeated drawing of the dark crimson marble was secretly telling me that he was sexually involved with another woman. But who was she? The answer was not long in coming.

"Just as often as my husband would draw the telltale marble from the bag, my best girlfriend would draw a marble of the same color.

"How could they do this to me? It was difficult, but I exercised a great deal of self-control during that evening. I didn't want to become emotional, I wanted to think the matter through in a rational manner. Regardless of Ralph's wandering, I wanted to save our marriage.

"I thought that evening would never end. I was on pins and needles until the last guest left, so that I could perform the Magic Ritual of Psychic Game One."

HOW CLAUDIA F. USED PSYCHIC GAME ONE TO WIN BACK HER HUSBAND AND MAKE HIS TEMPTRESS BEG FOR FORGIVENESS

After the guests had departed and Claudia's husband had retired, she sat quietly alone and determined that pure crimson, the color of fidelity and physical love, was the trait that she must encourage within her husband if she wanted to win back his love. But what about the temptress who was encouraging Ralph to meet her in an out-of-the-way motel?

"I knew that the first thing I needed to do was to remove the physical temptations that my supposed best friend was dangling before my husband. Instilling the spiritual qualities attached to the color of clear blue proved to be much easier than I believed possible."

Claudia performed her Magic Ritual and went to bed, convinced that she had saved her marriage. But even Claudia was surprised at the almost instant results her Ritual produced.

"I was just drifting off to sleep when my husband rolled gently against me and whispered, 'I love you. You're still the most desirable woman I've every met.'

"I'll never forget that night. It was as beautiful as our honeymoon ten years ago.

"Ralph hasn't looked at another woman since that night. He finds me so physically attractive, that there are times that I am slightly embarrassed over his attentions when we are out in public—but I love every minute of it. You should see the envious glances I get from women half my age who are wondering what my secret weapon is for getting a man so obviously in love with me. *Psychic Telemetry* taught me the secret. I doubt very much that they would believe me if I did tell them how I became so alluring to my Ralph."

Claudia felt like she was floating on air the morning after she had performed her Psychic Game One Ritual. She wasn't surprised when her telephone rang and the woman she had thought to be her best friend asked if she could visit Claudia that afternoon. "There's something I have to talk to you about," she said.

"I was very calm and polite when my husband's temptress visited me that afternoon," Claudia wrote. "I poured each of us a cup of coffee as we sat down to the table to chat.

"The adulteress broke into tears, and between sobs, blurted out that she had ruthlessly pursued my husband until he finally succumbed to her physical charms. I can remember her exact words.

'Can you ever forgive me for what I've done, Claudia?

Psychic Telemetry Games

'Please don't blame Ralph for what happened. My own marriage was on the rocks, and I don't know why, but I just couldn't stand it when I saw you and Ralph so happy. I guess I just needed the physical company that Ralph could provide. Oh, Claudia, what have I done?'

"Of course I forgave the woman," Claudia continued, "but before she left, I wanted to know what had occurred to make her feel so guilt-ridden over the liason she had created with my husband. This is what she told me.

'The scariest thing in my life happened last night, and I wasn't feeling a bit guilty over seeing Ralph. As a matter of fact, I was secretly planning my next rendezvous with him.

'When I got home from your party last night, I went right to bed. I instantly fell into a deep sleep, but I wish I hadn't. I had the most terrible nightmares. I kept dreaming that all kinds of terrible things were going to happen to me if I didn't quit seeing Ralph, and beg for your forgiveness.

'Just as I thought I was waking up this morning, I dreamed of a man in flowing robes lecturing me on what an evil person I was. I think that dream bothered me more than the nightmares.

'Oh, Claudia, I have such a guilty conscience that I don't know what to do. Please forgive me. I'll never, never become involved with a married man again. I've really learned my lesson. I've never felt so miserable in my entire life.' "

HOW TO PLAY PSYCHIC GAME ONE

This psychic game is a valuable occult tool. It can serve many different purposes at the same time, as you will soon discover.

The only utensils needed for Psychic Game One are a paper bag and an abundance of colored marbles. The marbles can be purchased at any toy store, or at a toy counter in a five-and-ten-cent store.

Psychic Game One as Entertainment—Though many people will deny the existence of ESP or other psychic powers, they become interested in any *game* that proposes to be a test of these powers. This Psychic Game has proven to be a wonderful icebreaker at parties.

The group of players is first shown the colors of the marbles, which will then be placed in a paper bag. Each player, in turn, announces which color marble he or she is going to draw from the bag (the bag is held at an angle from the player, so the marbles cannot be observed as the draw takes place). Each player is allowed five draws, and their accuracy is graded, in a lighthearted and humorous manner, against an ESP scale.

Five Correct Draws— The Psychic Prima Donna. Should be studied by the scientific community, or he's just darned lucky.

Four Correct Draws— The Psychic Seer. Watch out, Las Vegas! He knows all, and sees all.

Three Correct Draws— The Psychic Tenderfoot. He not only knows all, but he *tells* all. He only *thinks* he's psychic.

Two Correct Draws— The Psychic So-So. With psychic talent like this, stay away from the race track.

One Correct Draw— The Psychic Loser. Lock him in a room before he hurts himself.

No Correct Draws— The Psychic Clown. Ha, ha, ha!

Psychic Game One Used to Reveal the Players' Innermost Secrets—This is the game that Claudia used in the case history given earlier in this chapter.

In this game, you do not allow the players to declare what color marble they will draw from the bag. The players draw five marbles from the bag. The player with the most marbles of the same color wins the game, or can be graded according to the humorous ESP scale.

Psychic Telemetry Games

The vital difference between this game and the preceding game, is that the players will be drawing marbles whose colors will match the colors within their aura—they always do! Their hand automatically reaches for the marble whose color matches their personality most closely.

They believe that they are only playing a game, but you know that it is much more than a game. You secretly analyze the colors in accordance with the Color Tables previously learned in Chapter Five. The true character of the player is opened wide to your *Psychic Telemetry* gaze.

Psychic Game One Used to Enhance Your Sensory-Telemetry Powers—As you learned in a previous chapter, Sensory-Telemetry is the sensing and interpretation of vibrations, which gives you valuable information.

This game is designed to allow you the opportunity to practice this psychic skill in a gentle and comfortable manner, at your own convenience, and at your own pace.

Place ten identical blue marbles in a bag with one black marble. Without peering into the bag, reach in and withdraw the black marble. With a minimal amount of practice, you will soon discover that your hand becomes so sensitive to the blue colors, that you can *feel* the black intruder and withdraw it from the bag on the first try so often, that the mathematical odds against your achieving this success are astronomical.

A group of medical authorities, psychologists, and parapsychologists became intrigued with a former *Psychic Telemetry* student who could *feel* color with his hands. He is now being paid a hefty $30.00 per hour to play this marble game in a laboratory, while scientists attempt to discover the source of his psychic power.

THE PSYCHIC GAME ONE POWER RITUAL
THAT WINS UNFAILING CONTROL OVER OTHERS

Psychic Games used solely as entertainment must be laid aside as you now make ready to perform a Ritual that can bend the thoughts and actions of others to conform with your every desire.

Claudia turned her husband into a passionate and loving mate. She forced his temptess to beg forgiveness. You can do these same things, and even more, as you perform this miraculous Power Ritual.

Sit in your usual chair and perform your Ritual of the Two Pillars of Power. Visualize, within your mind, a picture of the person you wish to influence or control. Now hold within your hand a marble whose color corresponds to the aura color you wish to place in the individual's aura (in Claudia's Ritual, she first used a marble of pure crimson to command physical love from her husband).

If the person whom you are going to influence is a male, the marble should be held in the right hand. If a female, the marble should be held in the left hand.

Be confident of success as you repeat these words:

"____(Name)____ now bends to my will. My influence is total and complete. There are no obstacles that can hinder the success of my psychic mission, as the Universal Laws work unfailingly to fulfill my every command."

Your Guardian Genie already knows your desires. Send your Genie to the person you wish to control with the order that he "shake up" the mind of the person and make him receptive to the commands that you will shortly send.

The next step in the Ritual is to hold the marble in the palm of your open hand. Gaze at the marble without staring. In a calm but confident voice, say exactly what influence or control you are going to exercise over the person you have visualized earlier in your Ritual.

Continue gazing at the palm of your hand, forgetting that you are looking at a simple marble. It has now become a Psychic Power Cell.

A Psychic Time Clock resides within your abdomen. It will ring the alarm when it is time to bring your Ritual to an end. When you *sense* that your Ritual is at an end, bring it to a close by declaring:

"My will has now been done, and so it shall always be."

The marble used in your Ritual has become a powerful psychic force, and should not be used again in any Psychic Game or Ritual. Lay it aside and, when convenient, it should be buried in the ground.

YOUR PSYCHIC MARBLE CAN MAKE A FLOWER GROW

If you wonder how powerful an occult force your marble really is, bury it at the root of a flower and watch the results. They are amazing.

If the marble's color is one of the positive auric tones, the flower will become brighter, it will grow faster, and produce larger blooms than a similar flower growing beside it.

The negative auric tones will produce the opposite effect. The flower will become withered, stunted, and often die without apparent cause.

It's a wonderful experiment. Try it! You will be amazed as you observe the tremendous psychic energy that you are generating during your *Psychic Telemetry* Rituals.

PSYCHIC PARTY GAMES THAT SHOW YOU THE PAST, PRESENT, AND FUTURE

Psychic Party Games are more than just *fun*. Each game is designed to accomplish a specific psychic objective, but you are the only one aware of the games' psychic importance. Others play a game. You learn important details of the past, present, and future.

The games' players are not aware that they are using latent powers of Visual, Audio, and Sensory-Telemetry. They believe the games are all guesswork—but they inwardly hope that it is much more—and it is much more, but only you know it.

Watch closely as the games are played. You will be quite surprised to learn that many of your party guests have a great deal of ESP ability, but rarely know how to use it in a beneficial manner. At a later time, you can meet with these talented people and reveal *Psychic Telemetry's* secrets, if you choose.

Serious questions concerning the future will be asked during the games, and many of these important questions will receive frivolous answers. Other questions will receive extremely accurate prophecies of the future. You will intuitively sense the correct and incorrect answers to questions that are asked during the games.

PSYCHIC GAME TWO

This game is designed to utilize Sensory, Audio, and Visual-Telemetry powers. It gives you an excellent opportunity to practice your abilities, and at the same time gives you immediate feedback as to your psychic accuracy.

The game is played with any number of players. Each player writes a question on a piece of paper. The paper is then folded and placed in an envelope, which the player will now seal.

On the outside of the envelope, the player now writes a coded identification known only to him, e.g., ABC, 123, H20, etc. When all envelopes have been marked with the secret identification, they are gathered together.

Each player should now be given a different envelope, making sure that no player receives his own envelope. Without opening the envelope, each player is given five minutes to write the answer to the sealed question on the *outside* of the envelope.

As the host or hostess of the party, you will probably need to encourage the players. Simply state that whatever enters the mind of the player is probably the answer to the sealed question, and should be written on the envelope. "And if it isn't, remember, it's only a game!" you explain.

At the end of five minutes, the envelopes should be returned to their originators. The answers on the outside of the envelopes should then be compared to the secret questions still sealed within. The uncanny accuracy of some of the players will be astounding.

Psychic Telemetry Games

I have an entire file drawer filled with testimonials from people who have played this psychic game just for fun. Even though the game was used as entertainment, they did ask serious questions, which they sealed within the envelope. The answers were so uncanny, that the advice was followed and found to be completely correct.

HOW IVAN D. PLAYED <u>PSYCHIC GAME TWO</u> AND FOUND THE WATER THAT SAVED HIS VINEYARD

Ivan D. wasn't in the mood for a party, and he certainly wasn't in the mood for games. He was just about to lose everything he had worked for so very hard for.

Ivan was extremely upset but, upon his wife's insistence, he finally consented to go to the party whose invitation she already had accepted.

"I might as well go to the darned party," Ivan told his wife. "I sure couldn't feel any worse than I do right now."

Ivan had saved money for several years until he could buy some California farmland and turn it into a vineyard.

When the land was finally paid for, Ivan planted hundreds of seedling grapes. They were just reaching maturity and would soon be producing a paying crop of fruit, when the bottom dropped out of Ivan's world. There was a shift in the water table, and the well ran dry. Since there was no water to irrigate the maturing vines, Ivan was in danger of losing his entire vineyard.

"It's easy enough to say, 'Dig another well!' " Ivan wrote. "But there's a lot more to it than that. It takes a lot of dollars to drill for water."

It looked like Ivan was going to go deep in debt, borrowing heavily on the land he had struggled to pay for.

"I thought the hostess at the party had gone off her rocker when she said we were going to play an ESP game. I was convinced that she was loony when she passed out envelopes and told us to seal a question inside."

The only thing on Ivan's mind was the money he would have to borrow on his land.

"Here I was ready to panic, and those darned fools wanted to play a game. I went along with it and wrote, *Will I find water?* and *Where?* on a piece of paper and sealed it in an envelope. On the outside of the envelope I marked 'COWS' as an identification. No one could have know that the envelope was mine, and no one could have guessed what I wrote on the folded piece of paper which was sealed in the envelope."

Ivan was surprised when he received his envelope back. On the front of the envelope was an arrow pointing to the top of the envelope with the words "42 paces" written next to the arrow.

"That supposed ESP message didn't mean a thing to me at the time. In fact, I put it out of my mind as a bunch of baloney.

"On the way home from the party I told my wife about the problem with the vineyard. 'That's it,' she yelled 'Dig a new well forty-two paces from the old one.'

"Which direction?" I asked my wife. "I could have them drill in a hundred places that are forty-two paces from the old well. They could drill in a great big circle."

Ivan went to bed with a troubled mind. The evening's ESP game was completely forgotten.

"I must have dreamed about the arrow that was on the envelope, because it was on my mind when I got up the next morning. An idea just sort of filtered into my mind. 'Could that arrow be a compass needle pointing north? No! That's silly,' I told myself.

"It was several days before the well-drillers arrived. By the time they did arrive, I thought 'Oh, what the heck!' So I measured off forty-two paces due north of the old well and told them to start drilling.

"I don't know a thing about geology, and I don't understand how it happened, but the well-drillers hit water at a level twenty-five feet nearer the surface than the old well."

That "stupid psychic game" made Ivan more prosperous than he had ever dreamed.

Ivan wrote to me later.

"There is always a demand for good California wine grapes and I get a premium price from the winery for mine. Believe it or not, I'm actually rich!"

HOW LEONA M. USED <u>PSYCHIC GAME THREE</u> TO WIN A VACATION IN HAWAII

Raising two children on her salary as a drugstore clerk wasn't easy for Leona M. There was enough money for the bare essentials, but vacations away from the city were out of the question.

Leona's dream was that sometime, after the children were grown, she could save enough money to have a vacation in Hawaii. But the possibility that the vacation would be at any time soon was dim.

"I knew nothing about Psychic Telemetry when I went to Joyce's house for the houseware party, but a game we played that evening was one I later learned was Psychic Game Three," she wrote.

"I really didn't think a great deal about the game until two or three weeks later when I learned that the neighborhood church was going to have a carnival, and that a vacation in Hawaii was going to be one of the prizes. I really wanted that vacation, but I thought that my chances of winning it were mighty slim."

Leona called her friend Joyce and asked about the Psychic Game Three. "Do you think I could practice that psychic game and get better at it?" she inquired. Joyce assured her that she could, indeed, become more proficient with a little practice.

"I practiced Psychic Game Three every night before the carnival," Leona wrote. "There were some great prizes being given at the carnival, but the only one I was interested in was Hawaii.

"There was a large barrel filled with envelopes. Some of the envelopes were empty; others held receipts for various prizes. But there was *one* envelope among the hundreds that contained a small piece of paper that said, 'Hawaiian Vacation.' "

Leona paid her dollar and thrust her hand into the barrel.

"I closed my eyes and started praying, 'Please let me win.' I kept running my hand through the envelopes. I was startled when I touched an envelope that felt warmer than the others. I clasped it in my hand. 'I know this is it,' I said right out loud. I opened the envelope as fast as I could. I just stood there crying. In my hand I held a slip of paper. It said, 'Hawaiian Vacation.' "

Leona became a sure winner by playing a psychic game, and you can too! There really wasn't any deep, dark secret involved in Leona's bit of good fortune. And she didn't win her trip to Paradise by chance. Without even realizing what she had done, Leona had learned to use her Sensory-Telemetry ability with great skill. And I'm going to show you how to do exactly the same thing.

HOW TO PLAY
PSYCHIC GAME THREE

Psychic Game Three As Entertainment—This psychic game can be played just for fun, but while your guests are playing this variation of "Button, button, who's got the button?" they, and you, are developing important powers of Sensory-Telemetry. Powers that can be used to win contests—just as Leona M. did.

You needn't tell your guests that they are developing psychic power. They can enjoy playing the game while you consciously and secretly grow in your Sensory-Telemetry skills.

To play the game, place in a paper bag one red marble for each player. Then place one white marble in the bag. Mix up the marbles by shaking the bag.

Each player then, without looking, draws a marble from the bag and holds it firmly in his hand so that no one can see the color of the marble drawn. The players then guess who has the white marble. Or do they have it? Is it the one marble remaining in the bag?

Lest your guests suspect your *Psychic Telemetry* power, act very surprised as you time after time correctly guess who is holding the white marble.

You really don't guess who has the marble. You *know* who has it. Simply relax and *feel* where the round white treasure is located. Feel for the answer exactly as you were taught in Chapter Four.

Psychic Game Three As An Individual Sensory-Telemetry Exercise—This is an easy exercise, and it has been used successfully by hundreds of students who wished to concentrate their psychic efforts on their sensory powers.

Just as in the preceding section, place one white marble in a paper bag. Pour approximately 20 to 25 red marbles into the same bag. The odds that you can draw the white marble from the bag on the first try without looking are a million to one. But forget the odds. The odds mean nothing when you are in tune with your Sensory-Telemetry, or *clear feeling* powers. You will defy all odds with your correct draw—not one correct draw, but two, three, and four correct draws in a row. Amazing? Not when you're using *Psychic Telemetry*.

THE PSYCHIC GAME THREE RITUAL

Sit quietly and relax. When you feel at ease, repeat these words three times:

> "I am attuned to Cosmic Mind, which hears me now. My right hand is sensitive to color and to vibration.
>
> "I command that the white marble be warm to my touch. And so it is, now!"

Reach into the bag with eyes closed, and withdraw the white marble.

Many readers will find this Ritual unnecessary long before the last chapter of this book. But until that time, it is a valuable tool that can be used until you feel completely comfortable with your Sensory-Telemetry power. As your skills develop, you will no longer need the Ritual. You will just feel what you want to know instantly and automatically.

ADDITIONAL PSYCHIC EXERCISES THAT ARE GUARANTEED TO MAKE YOU A WINNER EVERY TIME

Former students of *Psychic Telemetry* have written to me asking if there weren't simple exercises or games they could play, "just to keep in shape." As one former student wrote:

"When I began my *Psychic Telemetry* Rituals and Enchantments, there were specific material possessions and people that I wanted in my life.

"Within weeks I had everything I desired—*Psychic Telemetry* really does make miracles happen. I didn't need to work any more miracles, but I did want to keep 'in tune' so that whenever a miracle was necessary, I could perform it quickly.

"The psychic games and the exercises you sent me really filled the bill. In the first place, they were a lot of fun. But more importantly, they kept me psychically alert.

"How did I feel? I felt like an agile cat—ready to leap into a miracle on a moment's notice.

"I'd recommend that all *Psychic Telemetry* students keep the psychic exercises in mind and that they use them as often as possible."

PSYCHIC EXERCISE ONE WILL INCREASE YOUR POWERS OF SENSORY-TELEMETRY

That intuitive *feeling*, that *sensing*, or just *knowing*, is what Sensory-Telemetry is all about. It's something that you are using every day, and has increased in power daily as you have thumbed your way through this book.

This exercise will further increase your Sensory-Telemetry powers. Your feelings will now acquire new and startling dimensions. You will actually *feel* a color with your fingertips. As you touch the object, its color will flash into your mind with the same intensity as if seen with your physical eyes, wide open.

This exercise can be accomplished by two different methods. Either or both methods will equally enhance your powers of Sensory-Telemetry. Many people enjoy doing both exercises, alternating between the two.

Method 1: The tools required for this exercise are simple and easily acquired.

Take small pieces of cloth that are equal in size—as many different colors as possible. There should be *two* identical pieces of cloth for each color. Separate these pieces of colored cloth into two piles.

Psychic Telemetry Games

Sit comfortably at a table, with the cloth in two piles before you. Have on the table *one* saucer for each color represented. The piles of cloth and the saucers should be located on the table before you in a manner that will make them easily reached.

Now, with eyes closed, pick from one pile a piece of cloth and cover it with a saucer. Continue covering the cloth pieces until one pile is depleted. Each piece of cloth from the one pile should now be covered by a saucer. Open your eyes. Sit and relax for a moment before you begin the next step in this exercise, which will be done with your eyes wide open.

One pile of cloth has been concealed, the other sits in clear view upon the table. Pick one piece of cloth at a time from the remaining pile and, without lifting the saucer, lay the piece of cloth on the top of the saucer that has the identical color concealed underneath. Then turn the saucers over. You will be amazed at how accurately you matched the colors of cloth.

Simply lay your hand upon the saucer and *feel* the color radiating through the pottery. As you *feel* the color, visualize it within your mind. One-hundred percent accuracy is not unusual after practicing this exercise a few times.

This exercise can also be a very entertaining party game.

Method 2: Using the same strips of cloth as in Method 1, mix together and place in a paper bag.

Relax for a moment, and then say, "I will now pull a red piece of cloth from the bag." Then pull a cloth of blue, green, orange, yellow, etc., from the bag. State what color cloth you are going to remove each time you draw. You'll soon acquire uncanny accuracy in this exercise.

An effective way to perform this exercise is to first state the color you are going to draw from the bag. Run your hand through the concealed cloths until your fingertips feel your stated color, and the color image is produced within your mind.

PSYCHIC EXERCISE TWO WILL INCREASE YOUR POWERS OF VISUAL-TELEMETRY

This simple exercise is guaranteed to increase your Visual-Telemetry power, though I am doubtful that your power needs to be increased. At this point in your *Psychic Telemetry* development, I rather imagine that you're quite expert in performing Visual-Telemetry. But if, as a former student previously stated, you desire an exercise just to "stay in shape," this one is ideal. It is ideal for you as an individual exercise, as you will soon discover for yourself. It can also be an exciting party game.

Take a regular deck of playing cards and shuffle them several times. Then lay the deck of cards on the table. Remove the top card, keeping it face down. Hold the card between the palms of your hands and, using your Visual-Telemetry, observe if the card is red or black. Do this with each card in the deck, laying the red cards in one pile, the black in another.

As your proficiency increases in *seeing* the red and black cards, you can vary this exercise by laying the cards in four stacks. Place all of the club cards in one pile, the diamonds in another stack, the hearts together, and finally the spades in their own place.

If you ever desire to demonstrate your Psychic Telemetry abilities, this in an exercise that will bring shrieks of disbelief from your observers.

This exercise with playing cards has undoubtedly been entertaining and psychically stimulating, but it is only an exercise and a game. Your real power comes from the many facets of Psychic Telemetry that you have learned in previous chapters.

Chapter Ten

Advanced Secrets of Psychic Telemetry For a Great New Life of Abundance, Health and Joy

Psychic Telemetry has shown you several methods by which you can bring your wildest dreams into a happy reality.

You no longer need to feel frustrated or alone. It isn't necessary to live in poverty—you can have every material pleasure. You can be healthy and strong. No longer do you have to be plagued with poor health.

You are now the captain of your own ship of destiny. Steer your ship to the ports of good health, prosperity, and eternal happiness.

HOW ELEANOR W. USED HER COMBINED PSYCHIC TELEMETRY POWERS TO BECOME A HEALTHY, DESIRABLE WOMAN AND WON THE MAN SHE LOVED

Eleanor W. was living in the northwest when I first heard from her. She had moved from one state to another, hoping that a change in climate would bring her relief from the constant illnesses which plagued her.

"I am just fed up with never feeling good!" she wrote. "If it isn't one thing, it's another. First it's my arthritis. Then it's my sinus headaches, watery eyes, allergies, and on and on.

"I'm really beginning to think I was born to be unhappy and miserable. I'm always feeling so poorly that it's hard to keep a friend, let alone find any man that would waste his time on a woman who's always complaining.

"Unless you've lived a life where you're always half-sick, you just can't realize how terrible it really is. Nothing every goes right.

"If I wasn't born to be miserable, someone has surely placed an effective curse on my life."

I sent Eleanor all of the *Psychic Telemetry* pamphlets on healing, and asked her to choose the method of healing that she felt the most comfortable with, and to at least give it a try. "You have nothing to lose, but a great deal to gain if you try *Psychic Telemetry* healing techniques," I wrote.

I didn't hear from Eleanor for three months. I began to think that she had either decided not to use the *Psychic Telemetry* healing instructions, or had made one of her frequent moves before the information reached her. When I did hear from her, the bubbly words expressed her "delirious" happiness.

"I'm so happy and full of energy, that it's hard for me to sit down and take the time to write a letter," she wrote.

"I'm busy every waking moment. It's sure a far cry from the times when I spent at least half of every day ill and in my bed.

"There's so much to write about, that my letter would turn into a book, but I did want to write to say 'thank you' for making my life worth living again.

"When I first received the healing pamphlets, I didn't bother to pick out the one method that appealed to me the most. I used them all—gem healing, color healing, healing enchantments, etc.,—I didn't want to take a chance on just one method."

Eleanor continued in her letter, "Along with the healing pamphlets, you sent 'The Advanced *Psychic Telemetry* Power Ritual.' That Ritual is amazing. Every time that I performed it, I felt like I was floating on air."

Psychic Telemetry healing techniques worked wonders for Eleanor.

"It was almost like a miracle. One by one, my illnesses left me. The first thing to leave was the arthritis in my legs and hips. The pain was bad enough, but the disease was crippling me. It was only with the greatest effort that I could walk around the house. Within days, I was out shoveling and pulling the weeds which had overrun my garden.

"Within a week, my asthma, allergies, and sinus headaches had completely disappeared."

Eleanor's illness had kept her so confined to her home, that she had had little time to become acquainted with her neighbors.

"Late one afternoon," Eleanor continued, "when I was working in my garden, the man who lived next door walked over to compliment me on my beautiful roses. It was love at first sight.

"Harry was a lonely widower who was a top executive at the aircraft factory. He obviously wasn't a millionaire, but he had more money than he could possibly hope to spend.

"Only two weeks after our first meeting, Harry and I flew to the Caribbean on our honeymoon.

"Needless to say, I'm delirious in my happiness. Regaining my health was miraculous, and I was so grateful, that I don't think I would have asked for another thing for as long as I lived. I couldn't believe that I deserved more.

"I am the happiest woman in the world, and would you believe that I have not had so much as a cold or a headache since *Psychic Telemetry* showed me the way?"

YOU CAN COMBINE YOUR PSYCHIC POWERS TO PERFORM A MIRACLE

Eleanor used several healing techniques to perform her miracle, and you can do the same thing.

Several techniques to perform the same miracle have been revealed to you in this powerful book. Many students, for example, feel the most comfortable with one method of healing, and use it consistently. Others vary their methods of healing, while other students will bring to bear their entire healing powerhouse upon the problem.

Performing more than one healing technique upon a problem does not cause one psychic power to interfere with the other. They work independently of each other, and cause no disruption to the psychic energy that you produce.

THE ADVANCED PSYCHIC TELEMETRY POWER RITUAL

It is difficult to adequately describe in words the power produced in this Ritual. It is somewhat different than the power you produced in your other *Psychic Telemetry* Rituals. A French countess, who is a *Psychic Telemetry* follower, described this Ritual as "The Seal of Approval from the Cosmic Mind." And perhaps it is.

This Advanced Power Ritual should be reserved for those special occasions when your psychic miracles are slow in reacting to your commands. This extra shot of energy will push your desires into reality.

First, stand straight against a wall. Your heels should be placed firmly against the baseboard as you begin the Ritual.

Repeat these words carefully:

"I am surrounded with the might and power of the Great Cosmic Mind.

"Every Nerve and Cell of my body now tingles and vibrates with the all powerful psychic energy of ages past.
"It is my will that will now be done.
"And so it is, both now and forevermore."

Now, take one step forward from the wall and remain standing erect. Let your head drop forward, keeping your chin and jaws relaxed. Swing your right arm backwards toward the wall and tap lightly with your knuckles three times, and repeat:

"I have power over all things physical."

Next, swing your left arm backwards toward the wall. After tapping lightly three times, repeat:

"I have power over all emotions."

Now, take the index finger of each hand and press gently at the bridge of your nose. The magic words to repeat are:

"I have power over all things of the mind."

The last step of the Ritual is to touch your chin to your right shoulder, and then to the left shoulder. While swinging your chin to the right and to the left, say with complete conviction:

"All is now done, and all is well."

Sit down and relax for a few moments when you complete your Ritual. You'll want these moments to savor the thrilling sensations experienced.

TEST YOUR PSYCHIC TELEMETRY ENERGY

Psychic energy is now constantly flowing through every bit of your being. There are two simple tests that you can perform if you want to experience a physical sensation as an assurance of your powers.

Test 1: Press the underside of your wrists together so that an "X" is formed. In but a few moments, you will feel a steady warmth stealing across your shoulders.

The warmth at your shoulders is created when you interrupt the general flow of psychic electricity that pulsates in every cell of your body.

Test 2: A sensation of warmth in the buttocks and lower back can be experienced as you cross your ankles. Press your ankles together in the same "X" manner.

A very good friend really puts this psychic energy to the test, and he did it simply as a test.

It was Thanksgiving Day in Denver, Colorado, with the weather registering below freezing, when Dewayne arrived at the University of Denver Stadium to watch the football game.

"People thought I was crazy," he told me, "but I was enjoying all the attention I was attracting.

"While the stands were filled with spectators shivering under their winter coats and blankets, I sat very comfortably in khaki slacks and a summer sport shirt.

"One lady leaned toward me and said, 'How can you stand this cold?' I just smiled. She would never have believed that my crossed ankles and wrists were acting as my own little psychic furnace."

HOW TO INCREASE YOUR TELEMETRIC SIGN LANGUAGE WITH THE MAGIC RECTANGLES

The secret which I'm about to reveal is very simple. And yet, it has escaped everyone but those who follow *Psychic Telemetry* techniques. The English philosopher who said, "Truth is simple, wonderful, and yet so wonderfully simple," was speaking of psychic powers such as the one you are about to learn.

You developed your Telemetric Sign Language in Chapter Four, and listed your symbols. By using the *Psychic Telemetry* technique that I am about to reveal to you, you can easily increase your Sign Language by four times.

Advanced Secrets of Psychic Telemetry

If you have been using ten symbols, you will soon have 40 at your disposal. If you developed your Sign Language to include 25 psychic words, you will now have 100.

All predictions of the future fall into four distinct classifications. Your visions of the future are in their nature either emotional, physical, spiritual, or mental. There is nothing else.

Using your Visual-Telemetry abilities, build this picture into your psychic vision:

EMOTIONAL	SPIRITUAL
MENTAL	PHYSICAL

Memorize these four rectangles and their meanings. And with eyes closed, divide your Visual-Telemetry mental picture into fourths.

Let's say that a bee in your Telemetric Sign Language denotes prosperity. Using the Magic Rectangles, it can mean four different things.

If, in your Visual-Telemetry, the bee appears in the top left of your vision, it is in the rectangle that denotes "emotional." The bee would therefore signify that your prosperity is coming from someone with whom you have an emotional tie. If the bee were in the lower left corner, it would signify prosperity through mental endeavors. In the top right of your vision, the bee would signify prosperity in a spiritual endeavor. In the lower right, prosperity would come from one with whom you are physically close.

See how very simple it is to expand your Telemetric Sign Language? Let's use another example.

Let's assume that a bell is the symbol of good news. Depending upon which quarter of your Visual-Telemetry vision the bell appears, it tells you to what the good news applies—good news from an emotional involvement, spiritual good news, mental good news, or physical good news.

From this point onward, interpret all of your visions in this manner, remembering that each of your symbols now has four meanings instead of just one.

You will soon discover that this Psychic Telemetry secret will increase the accuracy of your forecasts to a remarkable degree. And in addition to increased accuracy, you will discover that you can give an incredible number of predictions in a very few minutes—just as the young man referred to earlier in the book did on live television.

COLOR YOUR WORLD WITH PSYCHIC POWER

Color presents a psychic pattern. It shows a pattern of the personality, as you learned in the chapter on the human aura. Color is a magnet that attracts like vibrations unto itself. As it draws this like energy unto itself, it operates similar to an ordinary battery. It stores psychic energy until you flip a switch that allows it to send forth its electrical energy or power.

Color has an effect upon all people, whether they realize it or not. Color tends to influence everything around itself.

For many years, the color green adorned the walls of almost every United States hospital. It was the color of growth and healing. Green was not consciously chosen for these reasons, but the hospital administrators were intuitively guided to choose this color.

It is a rare cocktail lounge that does not have reds and blacks in its decor. Displayed together, these colors heighten the sexual urge and stimulate the desire for alcohol.

People are manipulated through the use of color in almost every facet of their lives, and it is the time for you to begin manipulating events and people with the psychic power of color.

Begin each day by determining what you hope to accomplish during the allotted hours. Do you want to attract prosperity? Wear brown that day. Do you want to stimulate passion when you go out on your evening date? If you do, stick to wearing red, black, or combinations of these colors.

Attracting those things you desire goes far beyond the wearing of colorful clothing. Do you have a child who has difficulty studying? Or do you have trouble concentrating yourself? Paint the walls of the room in which you study a pale yellow.

Do you have a hyperactive child? If you do, remove all of the yellow (which stimulates the mind) from your home and replace it with pale greens.

Do you want your husband to suggest a trip to the countryside? Wear clothing of a forest green color, and place throw pillows, etc., of the same color at strategic locations within the house.

If you're trying to bring honesty and morality into your home, decorate with pale blues and white.

Most *Psychic Telemetry* people are very successful in turning the tide to their advantage by manipulating colors.

HOW WILFRED B. USED COLOR TO SWEEP THE GIRLS OFF THEIR FEET

Wilfred B., a bachelor, was popular with all the girls, and he gave *color* most of the credit.

"I experimented and found that you could really influence people with color, and because of this, I had more girlfriends than I could handle.

"The first thing I did was to paint all of the walls in my apartment a true white. Then I bought ashtrays, throw pillows, throw rugs, and table cloths, etc., in a variety of colors.

"If Shirley was coming to my apartment and I felt romantic, I'd decorate with my red accessories. If Paulette was coming over and I felt like a lively discussion about the latest best-seller or a business problem, I'd decorate with bright yellow."

Wilfred later told me that color had changed his life.

"I not only used color to become the most popular bachelor in town, but I used it to win a better job, to draw prosperity to me, and to improve my health."

If you do not have your psychic colors memorized from Chapter Five, consult the Table of Colors and Psychic Definitions to color your world with countless wishes fulfilled.

You have also been exposed to the power produced by color in Chapter Seven, and have probably performed miraculous healing with your Ritual To Perform Healing By Color. One lady wasn't satisfied that one Color Ritual was adequate for her needs, and literally surrounded herself with Cosmic Color Power.

HOW FRANCINE E. USED COLOR TO SAVE HER MARRIAGE WHILE IT HEALED HER BODY

Francine E. was a miserable, middle-aged housewife who was not only ill, but was on the verge of losing her husband of 20 years.

"It was bad enough just having a heart condition," she wrote. "It slowed down all of my activities. My husband had always been affectionate, but my constant feeling of being tired had its effect. There was no more of that wonderful feeling of lying close to each other. He slept on the very edge of his side of the bed, and I did the same on mine.

"When I first read about *Psychic Telemetry,* I thought it was quite a coincidence that red was not only the color used to heal heart conditions, but was the color that could be used to stimulate passion."

Francine performed her Color Healing Ritual, and was soon cured of her heart condition. She was now physically active, but there was a wall between her husband and herself which she couldn't penetrate.

Francine's letter continued to speak of her efforts to gain her husband's attentions.

"Our marriage was definitely on the rocks, but I wasn't about to give up without a fight.

"The first thing I did was to redecorate our bedroom. The crimson bedspread and curtains look lovely. I even decorated the bathroom with black and crimson towels.

"Only a few nights after I had finished splashing our home with crimson colors, my husband put out his arm and pulled me close to his side."

You can rely upon color. Used properly, it can become one of your most advanced *Psychic Telemetry* tools.

IF THERE'S AN EVIL INFLUENCE LURKING ABOUT YOU, SALT IT AWAY

Since ancient times, man has recognized the need for salt in his diet and to preserve his meat. But salt was also recognized to possess occult powers. Throughout the centuries, salt continued to be a holy ingredient in the hand of the witch doctor, the saint, and the sage. The modern occultist has discovered that there is no substitute for salt in the exorcism of evil influences.

Most evil influences are created by the negative thoughts and hatred of unenlightened neighbors or acquaintances. But there are evil influences that are not just thoughts, but spiritual entities capable of disrupting the peace, harmony, health, and prosperity of those they prey upon. These spiritual entities are summoned by hate, jealousy, and envy. They are happy to do the bidding of those they have come to serve.

In Chapter Six, I instructed you in the methods to be used in cleansing a home of evil influences. But a more powerful and advanced technique of winning the battle against an evil spiritual entity involves the use of ordinary table salt.

Evil spirits consistently enter a home or other dwelling from the *north,* and when their work is done, they retreat toward the same direction.

If you are aware that evil influences in the form of spiritual entities have entered your home, you should go into action immediately and remove them from the dwelling by using any of the psychic tools learned in these earlier chapters of *Psychic Telemetry.*

When all entities have been expelled, place three pinches of salt at the northern corner of the building at frequent intervals. An evil entity will never come close to salt, which exudes a powerful vibration. This powerful vibration which flows from ordinary table salt causes pain and bewilderment to any evil entity coming upon it. In their bewilderment, these spirits will turn upon those who sent them, and justice is done.

Evil entities have been known to be successful in causing mental illness, depression, and a host of physical ailments. This need not happen—and it should not happen—when salt can be such a powerful psychic tool to prevent it. If an evil entity is bothering you, just "salt him away."

HOW JOSEPHINE L. USED SALT TO COUNTERATTACK HER EVIL ENTITIES AND WON

Josephine, her husband, and widowed daughter lived in a middle-class section of Kansas City. Things had gone well in the quiet suburban neighborhood until a petty feud began between Josephine and her neighbor.

"We had always gotten along well with our neighbors until our dog dug under the fence and destroyed a portion of my neighbor's much-loved flower garden.

"I didn't blame the woman for being angry, I would have felt the same way, but her fury was unnatural. She screamed and hollered like a banshee. She didn't even reply to our offers of paying for the damage done, and our promise that we would do our very best to replace each flower destroyed in the garden with one of like kind."

Josephine continued her letter by telling me that the woman was so determined to extract vengeance, that she began a study of withcraft.

"Things went from bad to worse," Josephine related. "My daughter, my husband, and myself were plagued with one illness after another. Our doctor even expressed surprise that a family as healthy as ours could so quickly become such frequent visitors to his office.

"One of my lady friends suggested that my neighbor had put a curse on my home and family. Anything seemed possible by this time, but unfortunately, my friend didn't know how to get rid of the evil which was making physical wrecks of my entire family.

"Months later, my daughter accidentally came upon a *Psychic Telemetry* pamphlet. By this time, all of us were at the end of our ropes, and would gladly have tried anything to remove the black curse which was hanging over us.

Advanced Secrets of Psychic Telemetry

"We read the instructions for removing an evil entity, but thought that they sounded too simple to be effective. We placed the three pinches of salt at the northern corner of the house, but we thought that our efforts would prove futile."

At the breakfast table the next morning, Josephine's family noticed that there was something different in the way that they felt.

"I can't find the appropriate word to describe how we felt the morning after we placed the salt at the corner of the house. The best word would probably be *relief*. We just felt relieved for some unexplainable reason."

Josephine finished her letter by saying, "Our health improved with each coming day. Right now we're in perfect health, and have all intentions of staying that way.

"The woman who was sending the evil entities to prey upon us is now confined to a state mental facility. I feel sorry for her, but she only received back what she was sending out to us."

A happy ending to what could have been a tragic story.

NO HARM WILL COME TO YOU IF YOU MAKE UNINTENTIONAL ERRORS IN PERFORMING YOUR PSYCHIC TELEMETRY RITUALS, ENCHANTMENTS, OR ADVANCED TECHNIQUES

You have learned many different Enchantments, Rituals, etc. But you should never be fearful that you have used the wrong one, or have mixed up its words or instructions.

The most that could possibly happen would be that the Ritual or Enchantment wouldn't work for you. A mistake would only be a mistake. Nothing would backfire on you.

The Cosmic Mind knows what you are attempting to do at every moment. Cosmic Mind judges the *intent* of your requests and works accordingly, even if you have made a slip or two in your Ritual.

If there comes a time when you can't decide which Ritual or Enchantment to perform, use the Advanced Psychic Telemetry Power Ritual which you learned earlier in this same chapter. You will soon sense other Rituals or Enchantments to use in performing your miracle.

HOW TO USE THE <u>PSYCHIC</u> <u>TELEMETRY</u> TRINITY, SAND-SULPHUR-SALT

The mystical origin of the power of sand, sulphur, and salt has been lost in antiquity. It was used by the ancient alchemist in his quest for gold. The Egyptian priest cast these elements into the flame that burned at the feet of the statue of Isis.

The African witch doctor sprinkled these three powerful ingredients at the doorway of the home of a newly deceased member of the tribe. It was believed that sand, sulphur, and salt would drive away any evil spirit trying to enter the home, but would also act as a beacon to draw those good spirits that would lead the newly deceased person into Paradise.

The American Indian medicine man used the three elements to not only drive away evil spirits, but also to heal the sick and give courage to the faint of heart as well.

SAND, SULPHUR, AND SALT REPRESENT AIR, FIRE, AND WATER

The power of sand, sulphur, and salt were believed to mystically represent the three basic elements of nature—Air, Fire, and Water. If one of these basic elements were missing, there could be no miracle.

In many ways these ancient mystics were correct, but the modern occultist has discovered that there are many other methods of performing the same miracles. The modern-day seer, at times, does not wish to be bothered with talismans, or mysterious tokens, as used by our Forebears. But there are countless others who place great reliance upon talismans, and they do work.

HOW ARIEL B. USED SAND, SULPHUR, AND SALT TO MAKE POWERFUL TALISMANS FOR THE PROTECTION OF HER FAMILY

Ariel B. lived in one of the toughest areas of Boston. Youthful gangs roamed the streets. Thefts, vandalism, and violence ran rampant.

"We were afraid to leave our home," Ariel wrote. There never was a day that passed without at least one of my children coming home bloodied from fighting.

"My purse had been stolen so many times, that whenever I left the house, I pinned what little money I had to the inside of my dress.

"If the house was left alone more than a few hours at a time, you could fully expect to find it burglarized on your return. It was like we were living among a bunch of half-crazed animals."

Ariel had been promised a good job in a nearby city, but that job wouldn't be open until the end of summer.

She knew that with her new job, she could afford to move away from her crime-infested neighborhood. But this was May. She still had three months of living in fear for the safety of herself and her children.

"I had attended a *Psychic Telemetry* meeting, where the power of sand, sulphur, and salt was discussed. I took a lot of notes," she wrote, "but I never did anything with them for awhile.

"One day, I dug my notes out of the drawer and did a lot of studying. I was interested in finding how to use the air, fire, and water elements as a means of protection from physical danger. I wasn't even interested in reading about protection from evil spirits. I think they would have been a welcome relief after what I had gone through."

Ariel purchased her ingredients. She mixed equal parts of sand, salt, and sulphur together and pour them into a small pouch.

"I carried my pouch everywhere I went. I never felt safer in my life. No one threatened or harassed me. Everything just seemed to change for the better overnight," Ariel stated.

"My pouch proved to be such a powerful talisman, that I made an identical one for each of my children. They escaped physical abuse for the remainder of the summer. The burglaries at my house even stopped, though there was little left worth stealing.

"Every time I left the house, I would put a pinch of my *powerful cosmic dust* (that's what I called the contents of my pouch) at every opening into the house—a pinch at every window, and at both doors. The burglaries stopped immediately.

"No one could ever convince me that the cosmic dust doesn't work. I'm living proof that it does work!"

I like Ariel's description of sand, sulphur, and salt as "cosmic dust." And here's how you can be your own powerful medicine man.

HOW TO MAKE YOUR OWN COSMIC DUST

The three needed ingredients are readily available, and very inexpensive if they must be purchased. The salt is regular table salt, available in every home. If the sand must be purchased, call any pet store. Small boxes are available for use in aquariums or bird cages.

Sulphur is also easy to acquire. If you live in the city, sulphur can be purchased at any hobby store that sells chemistry sets for children. In rural areas, you can purchase sulphur at any feed-and-grain store.

When you have your ingredients before you, place a level tablespoon of each into a bowl and mix well. Your cosmic dust should then be placed in any suitable container—a pouch or small bottle is excellent.

You may feel that three tablespoons of cosmic dust isn't enough. When you only use a pinch at a time, three tablespoons of dust lasts a long time.

Many people find that it isn't practical to carry their cosmic dust in a small bottle or pouch. I suggest that you acquire a small pill box at any drug store in which to carry your cosmic dust.

HOW TO USE COSMIC DUST AS AN ADVANCED PSYCHIC TELEMETRY TECHNIQUE

Ariel B. used her cosmic dust as a talisman for self-protection, and for the protection of her home. You can do this very same thing, and be very effective. For protection from harm, carry small amounts of cosmic dust on your person at all times.

A public service nurse, who is also a follower of Psychic Telemetry, carries cosmic dust on her person at all times, but for a very different reason than Ariel.

The nurse works with patients suffering from contagious diseases. She is in constant danger of picking up a germ or virus and becoming infected herself. She wrote to me not long ago. Her letter ends with glowing praise for protective cosmic dust.

"The average length of time that a nurse can work in communicable diseases without being stricken herself is four months. I've worked there for two full years and haven't become ill yet. There is no doubt in my mind that my cosmic dust is warding off every germ or virus that could make me ill."

Your cosmic dust almost has a holy quality about it, but it can also be used as the opposite.

If you have a desire to bring good fortune to any person, place or thing, sprinkle it with a pinch of your cosmic dust and watch all of the good things happen.

If, on-the-other-hand, there has been a person or a place that has not treated you well, sprinkle a pinch of cosmic dust there also. You'll soon see that circumstances arise where punishment is swiftly dealt out to fit the crime.

GENE H. SPRINKLED COSMIC DUST AT THE DOOR OF THE MAN WHO CHEATED HIM. THE BUILDING BURNED DOWN

Gene H. was an average guy who had gone into debt to purchase a luxury car that he really couldn't afford.

Gene was ecstatic as he drove his auto from the showroom floor. "It's only car I ever wanted," he leaned over and whispered to his wife.

Gene's joy was short-lived. His auto turned out to be a lemon. Everything that could possibly go wrong, did. He had his auto back to the dealer's service department every week. One thing would be fixed, then something else would go wrong.

"It was bad enough buying a lemon," he said, "but what made everything worse was the constant arguing I had to go through to get the car fixed.

"One day I had finally had it. The part needed to repair my engine wouldn't be in for a week, and I was going to have to leave it there because I couldn't drive it. I was furious!

"I walked out the door of the service department and threw a pinch of cosmic dust on the floor. I had only gone a few steps before I heard an explosion.

"For some unexplainable reason, an electrical short of some type had caused the auto paint to explode.

"No one was injured, fortunately, but all of the cars that were parked in the garage during the ensuing fire were destroyed.

"The dealer, of course, replaced all of the cars destroyed in the fire. My replacement auto isn't a lemon. It's a real beauty, and trouble-free.

"My cosmic dust saw another justice done," Gene said. "Because the paint was stored incorrectly in the garage, the insurance company refused to pay for the damages incurred. Every cent came right out of the dealer's pocket. Maybe he'll think twice before he treats anyone so unfairly again."

STRIKE IT RICH WITH YOUR NEW PSYCHIC TELEMETRY POWERS

Now nothing can stop you from enjoying complete contentment. Your life can now be filled with happiness, wealth, good health, and success.

This book has offered you the methods and techniques to work miracles. You know *how* to make *Psychic Telemetry* work. *Why* it works is unimportant. You are looking for results and you've found them.

Join the select few—the few happy people in this world. The happy people who have everything their hearts desire. Bask in the admiration of others as you live a lifetime of wealth, power, and love.